MW00634756

BREATHING AND QUIETING THE MIND

RAV DOVBER PINSON

RAV DOVBER PINSON

BREATHING & QUIETING -THE MIND-

THE JEWISH MEDITATION SERIES

THE EXPERIENCE & PRACTICE OF KABBALAH

 IYYUN PUBLISHING

BREATHING AND QUIETING THE MIND © 2014 DovBer Pinson. All rights reserved. No part of this book may be used or reproduced in any manner whatsoever without written permission except in the case of brief quotations embodied in critical articles and reviews.

Published by IYYUN Publishing
232 Bergen Street
Brooklyn, NY 11217

http:/www.iyyun.com

Iyyun Publishing books may be purchased for educational, business or sales promotional use. For information please contact: contact@IYYUN.com

cover and book design: RP Design and Development

pb ISBN 978-0-9890072-1-4

Pinson, DovBer 1971-
Breathing and Quieting the Mind: Jewish Meditation, Vol.1
1.Judaism 2. Spirituality 3. Philosophy

ב"ה

DEDICATION
IN MEMORIAM

—— of ——

OUR BELOVED

ZAKI AND EMMA
AND SAMY SAFDIE

ז״ל

Dedicated
*by their Children and Siblings*שיחי׳

MAY THIS BOOK BE A SOURCE OF MERIT TO THEIR SOULS

///

IN GRATITUDE

—— *to* ——

MR. & MRS. STEPHEN & SUSAN POLIS-SCHUTZ'שיח

&

THEIR SON, YONAH/JORIAN POLIS-SCHUTZ'שיח

—— *to* ——

DR.'S HANNA & MORDECHAI WOSK'שיח

—— *and to* ——

MR. STEVEN (MOSHE) HAZAN'שיח

with great appreciation for their continued support.

MAY THEY EXPERIENCE SHEFA BRACHOT,
ABUNDANCE OF BLESSING,
IN A REVEALED AND EXPANSIVE WAY ALWAYS.

YASHER KOACH

to

ARTHUR KURZWEIL ‏שיח'‏ & EDEN PEARLSTEIN ‏שיח'‏

&

A HEARTFELT NOTE
OF GRATITUDE & DEEP APPRECIATION

——— *to* ———

INGRID ARIA LATMAN ‏שתח'‏

**FOR THEIR TREMENDOUS EFFORT
AND DEDICATION TO THE TEXT**

MAY THEY BE BLESSED WITH ALL GOOD, IN ABUNDANCE
& IN A REVEALED MANNER

L'ZCHUS
in merit of

INGRID'S GRANDPARENTS:
YOSEF BEN ABA Z"L, CHANA MIRIAM BAS YITZCHAK Z"L,
LEAH BAS DAVID Z'L & YITZCHAK & YETTA, ZALMAN & ELKA,
ABA & CLARA, DAVID & ANA

TABLE OF CONTENTS

NOTE TO THE READER

//

IN THE PURSUIT OF WISDOM, THERE IS THEORY AND THERE IS PRACTICE. There is information and there are techniques of transformation. On the informational side, there are many books dedicated to exploring the underlying principles of Kabbalah and deeper dimensions of Torah. Few have chosen, however, to explore the actual experience of Kabbalah and spiritual practice; the transformational side. As such, I present you with this text. Not merely interested in what the great sages and Tzadikim, the "Righteous Ones", taught, but rather, what they did.

What were the techniques they used to become the people they were? What was the 'magic' that transformed ordinary people into extraordinary teachers? Of course, it goes without saying that a lot of hard inner-work, deep commitment to Torah, patience, perseverance and choosing to live large is essential, but was there something else? What were the actual practices used by the sages to expand their awareness and open their hearts? This subject matter is of primary interest and will be, G-d willing, explored in a thorough and accessible manner throughout the following pages.

Torah-based meditation practices are many. They run the gamut from simple to complex and open up a wide spectrum of states of consciousness available to the humble practitioner. A short list of meditations would include a diverse array of practices ranging from methods to empty the mind of all thoughts to filling the mind with chosen thoughts, from arousing emotions to transcending emotions, from visualizations to verbalizations, from external isolation to inner solitude, from silence to song, from self-expression to self-negation, from simple breath practices to complex transmutation of letters.

This book is the first volume to be released in a series. Each volume will explore a particular variety of meditations and spiritual practices as handed down to us by our holy teachers. Their mystical teachings will be clearly explained and made accessible and user-friendly. Each volume will follow a theme, such as: "Visualization and Verbal Techniques", or "From Silence to Song".

Due to the all-encompassing scope of Torah-based spirituality, these individual volumes contain much more than most books on meditation in its classic definition. For while Torah-based spiritual practices include many classic meditative techniques, they also include a variety of ways of relating to sacred text, attaining deeper faith, using music and song, and finding guidance on even the most mundane acts such as eating, sleeping and conversing. No aspect of life is left out.

The particular book in your hands is focused on two simple practices: basic breathing techniques and uncomplicated methods of quieting the mind, thereby freeing one from the perpetual deluge of disjointed, unconscious thoughts and self-obsessed internal monologue.

There is the conscious mind, which for the most part is somewhat under our control, and there is the unconscious mind, which seems completely out of our control. Breathing is related to the unconscious mind, as it is an involuntary act; we breathe without thinking about it. But breathing is also one of the very few unconscious biological processes that we can affect easily with our conscious mind; we can freely choose to hold our breath or to breathe more deeply. This creates a biopsychic feedback loop in which we are able to use our conscious mind to affect a physical process, which in turn will affect our unconscious mind. In other words, when we become aware of our breath, we can voluntarily improve the quality of our breath, thus linking our conscious mind to our unconscious mind. In this way, we may slowly gain control over the untamed and feral unconscious mind.

Both of these practices are quite easy to master with persistence and patience, and they are accessible to one and all. Little knowledge of Hebrew is needed and only an elementary knowledge of Torah wisdom is sufficient. All original texts quoted are in translation.

The sequencing of the books in this series moves from the more simple to the more complex, rather than following a chronological order. However, it must be pointed out that simple does not mean less meaningful or transformative. In fact, it is often that the most profound truth lies right before our very eyes, and it is we who are in need of changing our perspective in order to reveal the depths of what has always been there, just waiting to be noticed.

CHAPTER 1

ANSWERING THE 'WHY' OF LIFE

WE ARE LIVING IN VERY INTERESTING TIMES. The world at large, and the human being in particular, are going through major transformations. There is a shift inward. As a result of current technology, the world is becoming increasingly smaller and more interconnected. Due to the evolving sciences, from astro- to quantum-physics, our understanding of the world is becoming more integral, organismic, and unified. On an individual level as well, we are all being positively forced to seek out and discover any sliver of unity that resides within our own splintered psyche.

A UNIFIED WORLD

Within the past hundred years our empirical understanding of the world has shifted from an extremely dualistic view of reality, characterized by a subject observing an object, to a very non-dual paradigm. Scientifically speaking, we now understand that there is a deeper relationship between the observed and the observer; the perceived divisions between the object and subject are radically collapsing and essentially morphing into a giant unified nexus.

With every passing day we are inching closer to the revelation of the Ultimate Unity of the Creator and Creation. Though there are many who claim the world to be moving backwards towards a more primitive era, or at best, stabilizing, the world is actually moving forward on a progressive path, manifest on an internal level. Time continuously spirals forward and upward, from Creation to Redemption, from past to future. The question is, are we?

The choice is ours whether we respond in kind to the developmental trajectory of the world around us and spiritually evolve, which ultimately we will as this is the very Divine design for creation, or we can stand on the existential sidelines while the rest of the world transforms around us. For we do have the option to progress only physically by living longer lives and generating more material wealth, while simultaneously remaining impoverished of spirit. Sadly, this past century has proven that advanced technology can be used to destroy more lives than it benefits and rationality can breed more prejudice than it extinguishes. The choice is ours.

The good news is that humanity is slowly showing signs of choosing to expand its spiritual consciousness. As we become more tangibly aware of other peoples and places via the internet's globalizing effect on the world, we are increasingly more aware of plights and perspectives other than our own. We are becoming more sensitized to the ultimate reality that we are all in this together.

SOCIAL UNITY

As above, so below. As our knowledge increases concerning the inner-workings of the world around us, both cosmically and environmentally, so too does our understanding deepen concerning these dynamics on the social level as well. There is a more clarified grasp of the interconnectedness and interdependence between all people and all of creation including animals, plants, bodies of water and the environment in general. We are awakening to an understanding that the whole of creation is one unified organism.

A global village is indeed a reality today. We are all only six people, or even less, removed from every single person on this planet. With the rapid distribution of cellphones and the internet, people from all corners of the world are networking as a global society, stirring to life a sense of interrelatedness. This progress is moving us towards a Messianic time, a time of world Redemption, a time of ultimate unity, peace and understanding of the peaceful ways of the Creator.

Beneath the veneer of sensationalized media we are indeed moving, sometimes ever so slowly, towards a redeemed world. We have not yet arrived, but we are making incremental steps in the right direction. The mere fact that all branches of human intelligence, from science to psychology to physics to cosmology, are seeking more unified theories of integration suggests the deep pull towards this Ultimate unity.

REVEALING OF THE HIGHER & LOWER WISDOM – 1740- 1840

These dramatic modern-day shifts can be traced back to the elimination of a splintered sense of world geography and typography. Not so many years back, it was quite rare for a person to ever venture outside of his birth-town. With the introduction of quick and convenient travel — first by train, then car, plane and now virtually — a global consciousness was born. With the awareness of those living in far off corners of the world, we now possess a stronger identification with the other. All this began with the locomotive.

In the first book of Torah, *Bereishis* (lat. Genesis), it speaks of the Great Flood. The Torah says, "In the 600th year of Noah's life... all the fountains of the great depth were broken apart, and the windows of heaven were opened..."(*Bereishis*, 7:11).

Upon this verse, the *Zohar*, which is the primary text of Kabbalah teaching us the inner wisdom of the Torah, offers: "[This means that] in the year 600 of the sixth [millennium], the gates of wisdom Above and the wellsprings of wisdom Below will be opened. Then the world will prepare to enter the seventh [millennium], just as a person prepares himself toward sunset for the Shabbat" (*Zohar 1*, 117a).

In the Gregorian calendar, the 600th year corresponds to the time period between 1740 and 1840. During this time, both Higher and Lower wisdom began to be more profoundly revealed.

HIGHER WISDOM

In terms of Higher Wisdom, the 1740's saw the spreading of the teachings of the four most important Kabbalists, with each one starting his school of thought. They were all, in their own way, innovators and creative geniuses of the inner teachings of the Torah.

Within nearly twenty years of one another, these four

great sages were born: the *Baal Shem Tov* in Ukraine, the *Rashash* in Yemen, the *Ramchal* in Italy, and the *Gra* in Lithuania.

The *Baal Shem Tov,* Rabbi Yisrael ben Eliezer, was born in 1698 in what is today the Ukraine. He was no less than the founder of the Chassidic movement. The most important and innovative spiritual master of his time, he single-handedly transformed and revived Judaism. Today, more than half of Torah-committed Jews count themselves among his followers. The Baal Shem Tov's life, teachings and practices will be explored in detail in the pages to come.

The *Rashash*, Rabbi Shalom Sharabi, was born in1720 in Senna, Yemen. He eventually settled in Jerusalem, heading the Kabbalah Yeshivah there. He was the most important figure in terms of understanding the *Kavanos,* "Divine inner intentions" when praying, and advanced students worldwide still ponder this great teacher's every word, and pray using his special prayer book.

The *Ramchal*, Rabbi Moshe Chaim Luzzato, was born in 1707 in Padua, Italy. He was a profound poet and philosopher, writing many books on Kabbalah, ethics, logic and philosophy. His teachings are still read every day by thousands of students around the world.

The *Gra*, Rabbi Eliyahu, was born in 1720 in Vilna, Lithuania. He became a leading Torah authority of European Jews. Today, he is universally accepted as one of the great Torah giants of all time and the effect of his teachings are felt across all streams of Jewish thought.

The year 1740 was a year in which they were all alive and teaching in full-force.

LOWER WISDOM

Around 1840, the culmination of the 600th century, both England and the United States first successfully began using the steam locomotive. This time period helped fuel what is referred to as *The Second Industrial Revolution* and the beginning of the modern scientific explosion, the latter of which was only fully felt in the 20th century.

The locomotive unified the continent of the Americas, as well as the island of Britain. This was the beginning of stripping away the more restrictive geography of the past, where a person lived and died within the radius of a few miles. Of course, this was only the beginning. From there we moved on to cars, to planes, to space shuttles, and now to cell phones and the world wide web. Slowly, and in due time, we are forming the skeletal, circular, and nervous system of a truly unified planet.

For the past few hundred years, and more specifically in the past hundred years, the world has seen an escalation in technological innovation and application. There has been an explosion of scientific wisdom. These are all within the wisdom of the below, the wisdom of creation.

A SENSE OF EMPTINESS

The Lower Wisdom has been revealed and so has the Higher, and yet, they both need to be fully aligned for true integration to occur. The Higher wisdom needs to be revealed to all and assimilated into the very way we think as human beings; that has not yet occurred. Moreover, not only does there need to be an assimilation of such wisdom as information and intellectual stimuli, but also, and most importantly, as tools and techniques to be utilized and experienced in the course of our transformational process.

Until this happens, the situation is as follows: Despite the historic awakening toward the ultimate unity that permeates all, modern man is left with a gnawing sense of existential emptiness. The global becomes local, and yet man still feels this troubling loneliness, alienation and deep-seated frustration.

As the turn of the 20th century ushered in a period of great hope for humankind, there was a paradoxical phenomenon of some of the most barbaric atrocities recorded in human history. From Stalin to Hitler, including two World Wars, atrocities occurred across the globe. As a result of such large-scale horror, humanity is currently in a state of collective shock. We have not yet fully processed the great losses we have endured.

And so now we have moved into the 21st century, where personal computers reign and there is instantaneous pan-global connection and communication. Breakthroughs in science and technology are increasingly rapid. We have discovered more about the physical universe in the last hundred years than the past thousand years. And after having amassed such a vast knowledge of the cosmos, learned to manipulate the tiniest of cells, flown to the moon and probed the depths of the ocean, so many of us still feel a nagging vacuity; something terrible is amiss.

On the one hand, we are moving towards living in greater accordance with the oneness that extends to all in our global village. There is an excitement in the air and a sense of our innate human potential to break down boundaries that do not serve us as we move toward a more cohesive state of interconnectedness. This carries with it a tremendous scientific, spiritual, intellectual and emotional relevance and responsibility.

On the other hand, we continue to grapple with alienation, exile and the recognition that something is missing or out of alignment. And that is because the unity we seek is much deeper and more profound than mere external observational unity. Our soul, our inner essence, yearns to experience this unity, and not merely to know of it intellectually.

What we so desire on the deepest level is to actually experience the Source of All Unity not simply from the outside through detached observation, but from within an authentic encounter, through a dynamic relationship. We are subconsciously demanding the manifestation of the Creator's unity within the world. Via observation, the object and subject are unrelated; via experience, they are One.

This call resounds as a response to the depth of connection we so desire. Our essence, which is our soul, yearns for its own revelation within the setting of the Source of unity. Our soul responds to the need to bring together subject with object.

Within the current deluge of digital data, where with one click of a mouse almost all information is instantaneously available, we now search for ways to apply this information for conscious transformation, evolving what we know into what we do.

When we are graced with such a face-to-face contact with unity, quite different from when it is left in informational and observational form, we receive a taste of wonder, passion, awe, and love. This encounter culminates in a subtle ecstasy and inner rapture of *D'veikus*, an "experience of unity with the Source of all life".

INNER HUNGER

We are all hungry and thirsty, but in the words of the prophets, we are "Not hungry for bread, and not thirsty for water, but rather (we are hungry and thirsty) to hear the word of Hashem, G-d."

Bread and water merely satisfy physical hunger, but we cannot fill our internal emptiness with physicality. We can make an effort to accumulate more possessions, but this lack will only increase with every new physical acquisition we substitute for the real nourishment.

Power, money, clothes, cars, bigger houses, excess food, these are all externalities and therefore cannot quench an inner desire. We try to fill our voids with these commodities, sometimes even sacrificing our lives for them. And still, the emptiness prevails and worsens. The more we try to feed our spiritual hunger with material trappings, the emptier we will feel. That is because it is through the fulfillment of one's desire that one's vessel of desire expands. As the vessel expands, so too does the feeling of yearning, along with the sense that one's appetite is never satiated.

This is true in both the realm of the physical and the realm of the spiritual. However, with spirituality, this dissatisfaction does not create a state of lack, on the contrary it raises an awareness that we can receive much more than we previously were able to contain and we are now capable of being much better than the people we previously thought ourselves to be.

THE HOW AND WHY QUESTIONS

The fundamental mistake is that we exchange the substance of reality for the excitement of the chase, we trade the *why* for the *how*; we seek objects instead of subjects. All of the unimaginable breakthroughs we have been privy to only help to answer the how of life: how life works, how the planet operates, how we are here — not the why: why does life work, why does it operate, why are we here? As our minds thirst for the how and our souls thirst for the why, we must couple the two.

The sciences do a wonderful job of explaining the how of life, and this information merits great value. Think of the consequence of one little toothache 100 years ago. The tooth would be pulled without means to numb the nerves! Moreover, it is part of the Divine plan for lower wisdom to be revealed in this era. This is a preview of the world redeemed, healed and whole. Yet the picture is not complete until the *why* of life is demystified, and here science falls short of providing this formula. As long as we focus on quantity without quality and on knowing without being, our emptiness remains.

We seek the higher wisdom. This wisdom not only explains the why, but also delivers the meta-story of the what, a sense of the inner map of creation. Science is natural law, it speaks of the shell, not of what lies within.

A good metaphor would be of two maps of the same city. One is a street map, the other a subway map. Though they indicate different paths via different levels, they navigate the same city. Science is like the city map of reality. Kabbalah is like the subway map; it goes underground and behind the scenes to realms invisible to the naked eye.

THE MORE WE HAVE 'WHAT,' THE MORE WE SEEK 'WHY'

The more material wealth has become accessible to people from all walks of life, the more frustrated we have become. The more we have, or could have, the more discouraged we have become with the magnetism of materiality. The more we collect, the more we seek to unshackle ourselves from our attachments.

We are collectively richer than ever before. We are more informed about the physical universe than generations past. We have amassed much more of the what, and we are left asking why. Why does the world exist? Why do I exist? The Zohar, in its *Hakdamah*, "Introduction", speaks of two types of questions: the *Mah*, "What", and the *Mi*, "Who". *What* is a lower form question, according the Zohar. *What* is a question of factuality, "What is going on?" Modern science can answer the question: "what is this world?" and even, "how does it work?" But this does not satisfy the *Why* and the *Who*. Why is there creation? Why are we created? Who is the guiding force of Creation? We want to know and intimately experience the *Who* of creation, the Creator.

We are in a generation where traditional truths no longer stand firm in the face of mass disillusionment. In a desperate struggle to hold onto something meaningful people grasp for straws, clinging to anything and anyone that offers some relief from their existential anxiety. It is for this reason that meditation and many other mystical and magical practices and systems are being popularized. As our collective belief in the One has dwindled, we have come to believe in anything and everything. The menu de jour of spirituality is a smorgasbord and veritable junkyard of useful and equally useless information.

Meditation groups are ubiquitous and each one is led by a so-called expert in the field. Perhaps, some are true masters of meditation, but many are not. There is no shortage of bizarre ideas, new-age gimmicks, so-called Kabbalah teachers, magicians and miracle workers happy to fill their bank accounts from humanity's spiritual deficit. Instead of spreading peace of mind and wholeness, these gimmicks and charlatans only foster increasing fear, anxiety and aching emptiness.

This spiritual vacuum underlies all success and progress made by modern man. If this void will not be properly filled, people will continue in their mistaken efforts towards false fulfillment. And as a cursed cycle and self-fulfilling prophecy, the more things humanity amasses empty of real substance, the more empty humanity will feel.

AUTHENTICITY

The mind and heart will forever yearn until their yearning is addressed from a place of authenticity. The objective of the book in your hands is to introduce Torah-based spiritual practices to fill the void within. To this end, this book will not stop at theory and history, but will present actual practices that are accessible in all ways.

The primary focus of this series is to delve into the practices of the sages, primarily post-Talmudic, spanning the past 1,000 years and to present their original teachings in English translation as a how-to guide.

These practices will help one fill their lives with meaning and substance. It is important to note that these practices are not intended to supplant the practice of Torah and Mitzvos. On the contrary, these techniques have been used throughout the ages to stimulate expanded consciousness, cultivate deeper awareness, and calm the mind, so that the Torah and Mitzvos one does do are more internalized, meaningful and transformative.

These ancient teachings are available to us now so that we too can transform the Torah we learn from bits of data processed by our info-oriented left-brain into experiential epiphanies reverberating on all levels of our holistic and integral being. In this way we are able to imbibe the elixir of the fruit of the tree of life, breathing it into our very lives.

SIDE EFFECTS

There are also secondary benefits of meditation in addition to the more exalted goals of discovering inner-purpose and experiencing oneness with the Creator. One may also increase their focus by freeing the mind from noise, both from without and within. In a stress-filled world, this is a life skill that brings relief. There are derivative physical effects from meditation including reducing migraines, lowering blood pressure, decreasing stress on the heart, and strengthening immunity. In addition, meditation promotes concentration and compassion. By dispelling the veil of man's prejudices, we are able to observe — moment to moment — from a place of healthy detachment and non-reactiveness.

The Hebrew word most commonly used for meditation is *Hisbodedus*, translated as "isolation", or being alone. *Hisbodedus* is a process of drawing one's awareness inwards.

Given the way the world operates, we are conditioned to derive our sense of being and identity from external stimulus. For how long can you ride in a car alone without turning on the radio? We are so dependent on environmental noise that silence makes us uncomfortable. To be alone and still is frightening for the majority of us. Meditation weans one from their dependency on the external and redirects one's focus inward.

As King Solomon once said, "One against the other He created" (*Koheles*, Ecclesiastes, 7:14). There is nothing within the universe — in its current unredeemed state —that is either all good or all bad. Accordingly, there can be negative side effects from certain forms of meditation. Some researchers have found that suggestibility, depression, neurosis, paranoia and insomnia can be caused by meditation. This is understandable, considering the deep levels of one's psyche that one engages during the act of meditation, and ever more the reason why authentic practices taught by experienced teachers are needed. One needs to be grounded in a regimen of Torah study, specifically *Halacha*, "Law", as well as within a regular practice of *Mitzvos*, "day-to-day ritual and behavioral practices".

SPIRITUAL BENEFITS

Mentally, emotionally and spiritually, meditation is used as a device to attain inner liberation and loosen our intrinsic identification with that which is physical. From a spiritual vantage point, meditation is both a medium to encounter the Divine and experience transcendence, as well as a springboard for spiritual growth. In its most elevated form, it is a vehicle through which one ascends to ever higher and deeper realms and dimensions of awareness. Meditation is designed to focus one's awareness on the center of all reality, the Creator, and then to forge a conscious connection with one's deepest self in the place where the self meets its Maker.

DEEPER AWARENESS

The spiritual benefits of some of the deeper practices of meditation include such experiences as inner visions, ethereal images, clear guiding voices, altered means of perceiving reality. It is important to remember that our objective is beyond just tripping out. As the wise Chassidic Rebbe, Reb Mendel of Kotzk, once responded to a novice student who had come to him boasting of the exalted images he perceived while meditating: "Here, we must learn how to ignore and look past the images."

Our ultimate objective is *Deveikus*, cleaving to the Source of all life. The only way to make it to the Throne is by transcending even the beautiful imagery of the Palace.

One example of what can occur, although this is not our main aim, is the simultaneous observation of multiple dimensions of reality. We can normally perceive that there are three dimensions: length, width and depth. Why three? Three represents beginning, middle, and end. It is thus a perfect number.

The basic mathematical principle is that a point has zero dimensions, a line has one dimension, a plane has two, and a solid has three.

In the 1800's, a mathematical revolution took place. Mathematicians investigated curved geometries and found they could describe spaces with any number of dimensions and with all forms of curvature. Today, some theoreticians have proposed a way to jibe the general relativity theory with the quantum theory is to conjecture that the basic objects of this universe are not point-like particles, but two-dimensional strings and even higher dimensional branes. For this *string theory* to be mathematically consistent we need to suppose the strings and branes are vibrating in a space that has no less than nine dimensions.

However many dimensions there are, the question is: Can all three dimensions be viewed from a fourth dimension and be seen as one? After all, a three-dimensional object manifests all three perspectives at once. The answer is yes.

When the prophet Ezekiel experiences a mystical vision, he observes the chariots revolving and sees all three sides at once. He describes this prophetic vision and states that he saw angels with four distinct faces on each one of their sides: "The face of a man, and the face of a lion to the right....the face of an ox to the left....and the face of an eagle..." Ezekiel further emphasizes the fact that although they were in motion, "they did not turn as they went" (*Yechezekel* 1:10, 9:12-17). He perceived all dimensions at once.

We are embarking upon a new journey through ancient waters. Use these teachings and techniques to build yourself a strong foundation upon which your learning and practice will deepen and expand. These beginning meditations are accessible, practical and essential.

///////////////////////////////////////

CHAPTER 2

··

MEDITATION
AS LIFE

MANY PEOPLE HEAR THE WORD MEDITATION AND THINK:
Cave on a mountaintop, somewhere exotic and remote, person in isolation sitting cross-legged on the floor. In truth,
as will be explored further, meditation is not only reserved
for moments of isolation. Meditations, which plant seeds of
awareness and *kavanah* into the soil of our soul, are methods by which one can attempt to simultaneously focus and
expand their consciousness in order to live fully in the moment, every moment.

Considered as such, a meditative life is the aspiration of Torah-living, as its focal point is *Mitzvos* (sing. Mitzvah). Simply translated, *Mitzvos* refer to the commandments of the Torah. The root of the word *Mitzvah* is *Tzavta*, meaning "to connect". With each *Mitzvah*, we are invited to forge a deeper connection and realign ourselves with our Source. Through this act, a shift of consciousness takes place and one attains an awareness of living in the presence of the Creator.

There are two components of *Kavanah* that need to be present during the performance of a Mitzvah. One is the embodied awareness of the physical act of performing the Mitzvah itself. The other is the awareness of the Giver of the Mitzvah, the Creator. Kavanah is more than mindfulness. It is a reorientation of the whole human being toward the presence of the Divine in this very place and time.

Every action or exchange is an opportunity for a Mitzvah, a chance to connect. By extension, the opposite is also true. The inherent system of free choice opens the possibility of *Aveira*. While commonly translated as "sin", the root word in Hebrew is *Avar*, meaning "other side", connoting the idea of separation. As Mitzvah is conceived of as connection, Aveira can be understood as separation. In life, all of our thoughts, words, and actions bring about either connection or separation.

To walk the path of *Halachah* is to be in a constant state of connection with the Divine. Halachah literally translates as "walking". This is a linguistic hint suggesting that life itself is a journey and the practice of observing Halachah enables one to walk this path of Mitzvos with a sensitized awareness of the import of our actions and a heightened sense of love, connection and awe in the face of the Infinite One.

In this way, meditation is not a withdrawal from life and its fullness—although certain forms may engage in this for temporary periods. If practiced correctly, meditation empowers the practitioner to seal his or her spiritual practice with a deeper sense of self, a renewed appreciation for life in this present moment, and a perpetual awareness of the Source of all life. Meditation offers a new way of seeing and a deeper way of interacting with the Oneness of the Creator, moving beyond mere contemplation and comprehension into the experience of personal involvement.

Meditation gives birth to a kind of awakening watchfulness, stimulating a deeper awareness of the surrounding world at large and of one's inner world as well including every thought, word and action. This kind of focused and expansive perception allows one to behold and appreciate the limitless awesomeness of the world in which we exist.

ORAL TRADITION OF MEDITATION

Since much of the tradition of Torah in general, and the inner teachings of Kabbalah in particular, are based upon a vibrant oral tradition that is given over from teacher to student, very little was ever clearly written down in terms of how to practice the meditations that we will be exploring. This is information that the student would have received from his teacher directly. There is not much currently available in terms of how-to meditation guides from authentic masters of Kabbalah. It was only very recently, in the last hundred years or so, that some of the more profound teachers, such as the Peasetzne Rebbe and the Rashab of Chabad, began to provide treatises on the practices they taught. Even with these invaluable gems, our task at hand is a bit of a treasure hunt, collecting such scattered teachings from the various and often obscure texts and piecing them all together into a cohesive method and practice.

In a previous book entitled *Meditation and Judaism*, the Biblical and Rabbinic roots of meditation from the Torah, the Prophets, the Writings, and later, from the sages of the Talmudic period were documented, organized and explained. In that well-footnoted text, the ancient sources of the essential practices of Jewish meditation were acknowledged and analyzed.

The focus of this work is to delve deeply into the actual practices of the post-Talmudic sages from one thousand years ago to the present in order to offer their original writings in translation accompanied by an extensive explanation of what these writings mean and how are they relevant, resulting ultimately in the presentation of a contemporary and practical how-to-guide based on those teachings. A short biography of each teacher will also be presented, along with a basic explanation of their unique teachings. This will provide a basic intellectual historical context, which will help the reader better understand the actual teachings themselves.

Each practice will be presented in the original source text, translated into English. Each chapter will be concluded with a step-by-step guide to how to practice the meditation.

THE PRACTICES

The series as a whole will explore a wide range of spiritual masters and their practices. The scope of these practices encompasses the full spectrum of human experience including meditations directed to the intellect, the heart, the body and the transcendental dimension of spirit.

The methods include:

- HASHKATA :emptying the mind of all thoughts
- HISBONENUS :filling the mind with chosen thoughts
- HISTAKLUS :visualizations and inner light awareness
- TZIRUF :sound, letter permutations and prophetic ecstatic practices
- HISBODEDUS :seclusion, being alone, speaking freely to the Creator
- GEIRUSHIN :divorce from society and life
- DEVEIKUS :cleaving and sensing Divine oneness
- HISLAHAVUS :arousing emotions
- BITUL :nullifying self-expression

- NEGINAH :music and dance

- SHETIKA :silence practices

- YICHUDIM :Divine Names

- AYIN :emptying the self of ego

- CHESHBON HANEFESH
  :accounting of the soul, soul searching

- HEVEL :simple breathing techniques

Included above is a wide range of practices, some rudimentary and others quite advanced. There are some practices that demand superior knowledge, Hebrew reading skills and comprehension, and a general understanding of Torah and Kabbalah. The others are practices that necessitate mere basic human knowledge. To create order out of this vast body of wisdom, practices have been grouped together according to level of complexity.

As mentioned above, in place of one large mega-text with thousands of pages, notes, references and cross references, the practices will be divided into numerous individual books. Each book will focus on a specific set of practices. For instance, one book will focus on visualizations, another book on unifications of the Divine name, and yet another one on the art of letter combinations and head movements. These are just a sampling of the many techniques and spiritual technologies we will be exploring.

The current book is intentionally the first book in the series, as it is accessible to the novice and requires very little knowledge of Hebrew or even Torah in the classic sense. When a more complex idea is presented, it will be properly explained.

Breathing is the most natural thing we do, it is involuntary and innate. In the course of this work, authentic techniques for basic breathing exercises will be offered together with a very basic method of quieting the mind. These two practices, breath-work and quieting the mind, are being presented together due to the simple fact that quieting the mind is an essential foundation for any form of meditation or contemplative practice. Without a basic control of the mind, any method of more advanced meditation will be impossibly frustrating, and may end up doing more harm than good. The primary teachers of these two practices are the Baal Shem Tov and the Peasetzne Rebbe. Both of whom you will get acquainted with through their biographies and intellectual histories detailing and explaining their ideas and influence.

BREATHING & QUIETING THE MIND

The value of improving the quality of one's breath is an essential ingredient for beginning the path of meditation. In addition to its simplicity, conscious mindful breathing expands our humanness. We coalesce with the world surrounding us, thus feeling less alienated. We become more when our sense of distance from others lessens. We begin to view ourselves as an integral part of something infinitely greater than what we had perceived ourselves to be. We become more in touch with our deeper nature, a glimmer beyond the ego. Our sense of dependency on, or better yet, our interdependency with the world outside of us sharpens and becomes more real. We realize that we simply cannot be without the world around us. We become closer to other people, and hence, to life itself. Our capacity to love and our enthusiasm for life is tremendously enhanced.

HORSE THOUGHTS

Quieting the mind is essential as a foundational practice of meditation. The Russian and Polish Kabbalists, as well as other Jewish spiritual masters, speak about 'horse thoughts.' While monkeys were prevalent in the Orient, where the phrase 'monkey mind' came to life, horses were abundant in Eastern Europe, inspiring the phrase 'horse thoughts.' To the best of our estimation, a horse is always thinking about what is in front of him in this very moment. Whether it is a basin of water or a pile of hey, the horse is thinking of the basin of water or the pile of hey. As pathetic as it may sound, people often entertain 'horse thoughts' as well.

Imagine you decide to think over a particular chosen thought on your walk from home to work. As you step out of your house you bring the thought into your mind's eye, but immediately the first thing you see, hear, smell or touch pops into your train of thought. Let us say you hear a siren going off in the distance and your mind instantly wonders about the siren. You notice the clouds, so you begin to wonder if it is going to rain. This sets off a whole chain of thoughts: *Do I have an umbrella? Umbrellas are so expensive. I should really make more money. I don't like my boss* — and so on and so forth. The horse thoughts unravel and take over the driver's seat of your mind. In a short period of time, your mind has traveled on a wild ride of loosely connected destinations. The unifying point for them all is that not one of them was chosen and not one of them was the original thought you decided to think about on your way to work.

Most people think they choose their thoughts, when in truth — your thoughts choose you. "I think therefore I am," is not as true as, "I am what I think." Our minds are scattered and often without clear focus, they jump around like kernels of corn in a popcorn machine.

The scattered nature of the mind informs our words and deeds. How many times do we say something only a moment later to say, "I am so sorry! I said that, but didn't really mean it"? It seems at times as if the mouth has a mind of its own. The same is true with actions. How many times have you done something only to regret it a second later? In the words of our sages, "The wicked [those not living an integrated life] are full with regret."

Our prayers remind us: "Because of our sins we were ex-iled". Exile is not merely external, but deeply existential. Ultimately, it is an alienation from ourselves, within our-selves. Our thoughts, words and actions seem to float about with very little participation or direction from our conscious mind. They are in exile from our inner reality.

Our minds are the funnels through which we appreciate and interpret reality. Being that the mind seems to be at the mercy of the never-ending external trappings and the horse thoughts they bring on, it is recommended that a primary objective of conscious life be to take back the reigns of con-trol for this wonderful tool, the mind.

Integration of our inner thoughts and desires with our ex-ternalized words and actions is fundamental for effective living. This holistic integration is an alignment of will, pur-pose and goal.

The majority of us operate ineffectively because we are out of our integrity and therefore not capable of harmonious-ly orchestrating our physical, mental and spiritual energies. We are at odds with ourselves and lack a sense of alignment or center.

CENTERING

The word meditation is derived from the Latin word *Medi*, which means, "center". To meditate is to discover and align our thoughts, words and actions with our center of being, thus empowering and expressing, from our deepest depths, who we truly are in life. To meditate is to get in touch with our true self and inner nature, moving away from, or taking the psychic power back from the false self who manifests as ego and derives its identity solely from the externalities of life such as material possessions, honorific titles, or popular public approval. Ostensibly, if one's ground of being is outwardly dependent, it is logical to infer that the only interactive interface with the outer world is the carapace standing in place of self.

Through the wonderful practice of quieting the mind and observing one's thoughts the road to self-awareness is patiently paved. The ego is tamed through meditation enabling us to become observers of our own lives. From this vantage point, the meditator clearly observes the internal world, thus deconstructing the patterns and traits that dominate his life, and receiving the opportunity to correct them.

The byproduct of self-observation is self-assurance and self-esteem. Through increasing inner awareness and inner-directedness we are less at the mercy of external forces and whims and become more sensitive to what we truly want, and to what makes us truly feel alive and connected with the bigger picture. Through self-knowledge we avoid becoming what we need not be, and instead become what we truly are.

VERTICAL & HORIZONTAL EXPANSION

There are two spiritual movements: vertical and horizontal. A vertical trajectory of development is upward, horizontal is outward. Deepening a spiritual practice can either lead one up the vertical ladder or across the horizontal bridge. One who travels the vertical path learns to climb higher, soaring above and entering deeper within to activate their spiritual potential. With greater access to spiritually-heightened awareness there is the possibility of even attaining a measure of prophetic insight, beyond the normal range of natural psychic powers. One whose spirituality expands horizontally seeks to become more open, loving and sensitive to others, expanding their sphere to include more of life and all of creation.

The goal of Torah based practices is to expand in both directions, equipping the meditator with the tools and techniques to move upwards, inwards and outwards, to become higher, deeper and more expansive. In this manner, one's understanding of the Divine deepens, as well as the recognition of the connection between self and cosmos.

The practices work on two levels at once: Tuning us in more to the Creator, as well as drawing us closer to our own soul and that of others sharing this space and time. Spiritual sensitivity is augmented and interpersonal character traits are developed simultaneously raising one upwards while expanding outwards.

PART ONE

QUIETING THE MIND

PART ONE

QUIETING THE MIND

THE QUEST TO QUIET THE MIND

ANY SENSE OF INNER FREEDOM OR GROWTH demands that we gain some hegemony over our thoughts so as not to be at the mercy of whatever burps up to the mind. Not only are most people not in control of their thoughts, worse yet, even when a person chooses to think a particular thought, the mind has a mind of its own, attempting to shut out the intention.

Quieting the mind of the onrush of unwanted, undesirable and unconscious thoughts is the objective of the practice that will be explored in detail in this chapter. Learning to quiet the mind is learning how to separate one's thoughts, to learn to be able to isolate one set of thoughts from another, and to be able to observe your own self-thinking. This is a form of *Hisbodedus*, which is the classic Hebrew word for "meditation", from the root word *Badad*, "alone", separate. This is internal, a practice of Hisbodedus within the mind.

But before *Hisbodedus Penimi*, "internal isolation" is explored, let us begin with the external isolation and then move to the more subtle and internal forms.

In times past, the act of external isolation — roaming alone in the wilderness, separating oneself from society, leaving behind the noise of the city and the buzz of social life — was a prerequisite for the prophetic experience. In the Torah and the Prophets, we find the Patriarchs, *Moshe*/Moses, and many of the later prophets strolling the countryside as shepherds, isolated from mundane life.

Ever since the end of the prophetic age, mystics and sages, Chassidic Rebbes and Musar teachers alike have all advocated a kind of Hisbodedus practice. Go alone into the fields, away from the city, or even to a dedicated room to be alone with oneself and alone with the Creator. This is a practice on its own and will be explored in much greater depth in a future volume. Suffice it to say, there is a long and time-honored tradition to practice some form of Hisbodedus.

HISBODEDUS CHITZONI/ EXTERNAL ISOLATION

Separating from the world for a period of time is called *Hisbodedus Chitzoni*, "external isolation". The purpose of this practice is to literally remove oneself, once or twice a day, from people and to be alone with oneself and alone with G-d, preferably in nature. Being alone with our thoughts allows us to become more in touch with our deepest self and makes it easier to be one with the Source of all.

In this physical isolation from others we are more attuned to our inner selves, free to express deep desires, yearnings and aspirations as well as what hurts, troubles and pains. We learn to be alone with the Creator of the Universe as we are alone with very close, intimate friends.

RABBI AVRAHAM BEN HA'RAMBAM

In addition to the external act of isolation there are more subtle forms of Hisbodedus, mostly for the purpose of attaining heightened spiritual sensitivity and prophetic-like insights.

One of the earliest and clearest sources for this kind of meditation is from the writings of Rabbi Avraham (1186 – 1237), the son of Maimonides (Rambam). R. Avraham was born in Egypt when his father was 51 years of age. In 1204, when the Rambam passed away, young Avraham was still a teenager. Recognized for his brilliance as a scholar, he succeeded his father as the *Nagid*, "head of the Jewish community", and as the court physician.

In addition to his writings on Halacha, defending his father's positions against critics, and his commentary on the Torah, Rabbi Avraham's principle book was a spiritual manual for living written in Judeo-Arabic, entitled *Kitāb Kifāyah al-Àbidîn*, "A Comprehensive Guide for the Servants of G-d". Today, it is known by its Hebrew title, *HaMaspik L'Ovdei Hashem*. While we are fortunate to have this book on our shelves, the majority of its pages were lost.

HISBODEDUS PENIMI/ INTERNAL ISOLATION

In HaMaspik L'Ovdei Hashem, Rabbi Avraham speaks about external isolation and the need to cultivate a practice of being alone with oneself in order to nurture a more contemplative inner life. He also speaks about a practice called *Hisbodedus Penimi*, internal isolation within oneself. This is a form of isolation or discernment within the mind, where one learns to separate subtle states of mind from each other.

The work is to learn how to separate empty or idle thoughts from loftier ones until the mind is solely occupied with thoughts of one's Creator.

These two types of isolation, internal and external, are allied. The act of physically separating oneself from the day-to-day life and environment allows one to cultivate a more inwardly directed lifestyle of contemplation and centeredness.

Here is a quote from R. Avraham:

[excerpted and translated from, 'HaMaspik L'Ovdei Hashem']

"Being in solitude is one of the most elevated of all elevated traits. It is the path of the great Tzadikim. Through it, the prophets reached a level of revelation.

This in itself is divided into two: there is Hisbodedus Chitzoni, "external isolation", and there is Hisbodedus Penimi, "internal isolation". The purpose of the external isolation is to attain the awareness of internal isolation, which is the highest level in the ladder of revelation. And not only that, it in itself is the actual revelation.

Now we can say that this internal isolation is what King David prayed for when he said, "A pure heart create for me, O G-d" (Tehilim, 51:12)...And this is the purity of the heart and its refinement from anything besides the Divine...This, one attains through the nullification of the activities of the sensing soul of the person, completely or partially. And pushing aside the parts of self that goad one to other areas of life, and cleaving to the Creator, and using the intellect for Divine ideas and working with the power of imagination to meditate and think about His creation. Meditating on the wonderful majestic creations that all point to their Creator. Meditating on the vastness of the seas and the awe-inspiring and wonderful creatures within the sea. Or meditating, gazing and marveling the night sky, with all the bright stars…

To achieve this inner isolation, which unifies man with his Creator, the prophets and their students employed music and musical instruments. Music awakens and arouses…and purifies the internal from anything that is outside of Him…if only this would return to us speedily as it used to be.

This is the reason why the prophets and their students were inclined to external isolation since it brings one to internal isolation."

(HaMaspik L'Ovdei Hashem, Erech Hisbodedus. p. 177-185)

Hisbodedus Penimi is to be wholly attached to the Divine, divorcing oneself from any preoccupation with the mundane or trivial. This was achieved through first practicing Hisbodedus Chitzoni.

It is important to note that the great moralist and teacher, Rabbi Bachya Ibn Pakudah (11ᵗʰ Century), writes that in contrast to the philosophers of the world who champion Hisbodedus Chitzoni, the main act of Hisbodedus, he says, is being *alone* even when in the midst of a large community all practicing together with one *Kavanah* toward the Creator. This is worth more than all of the individual Hisbodedus of the world* (*Chovos Halevavos. Shar Ha'perishus,* Chap. 3). Although, he does also write of the virtue of Hisbodedus as a means to stay away from certain temptations (*Shar Cheshbon Ha'Nefesh,* Chap. 17).

Indeed, every situation is different, as the Rambam, the father of R. Avraham, writes: "A pious man should seclude himself and only interact with other human beings when necessary."(*Moreh Nevuchim,* 3:51).

_____

* However, the masters of contemporary Mussar do write that one should, as much as possible, literally separate himself from people, and to learn to "love being alone." R. Yoseph Zundal of Salant. (1786– 1866) *M'zkeinim Esbonen,* p.140. *Ohr Yisrael,* p. 30. See also: *T'nuas HaMsusar* 1, p 135. Rabbi Simcha Zissel Ziv of Kelm. (1824 - 1898) *Kisvei Ha'Saba M'Kelm,* p. 176. Rabbi Yitzchak Blazer (1837 - 1907) *Chocvei Ohr,* p. 176. Rabbi Alexander Moshe Lapidus. *Divrei Emet,* Chap. 13. p. 94 – 98. In the words of a 'classic Musar' text, "The secret to attain a love for Hashem is to (first) attain a love for Hisbodedus." *Reishis Chochmah.* Shar Ha'Ahavah 3.

It should also be pointed out that the Peasetzne Rebbe wanted to create *Chaburas*, "spiritually-oriented groups", where people would gather together from time to time with the intent purpose of learning together and helping one another grow, spiritually, encouraging each other when needed.

Many years later, the Chassidic teacher, Rabbi Klunimus Kalman (1751 – 1823), the *Maor VaShemesh* (a great-grand-father of the Peasetzne) taught:

> *[excerpted and translated from, 'Maor VaShemesh']*
>
> *"If a person desires to truly serve the Creator, and to create unity between the Divine Transcendence and the Divine Immanence with every action he does, he needs to separate himself from other people, not to connect himself with other people who are not appropriate; only, sometimes to connect with living Tzadikim in order to observe their holy work. The main idea is to practice Hisbodedus in his thoughts, separating himself, not so much physically, but internally from negative, mundane thoughts, and to continually meditate on the wonders of the Creator."*
>
> *(Maor Vashemesh, Terumah. p 253).*

It is not so much about externally separating from other people, although that is needed when one feels bogged down by distractions, veering in the wrong direction. It is mostly about finding the right community, to be in the right company of people who share common aspirations and life values.

RABBEINU YONAH OF GERONA

A contemporary of R. Avraham, the saintly Rabbeinu Yonah of Gerona (1194 - 1263), was one of the first leading opponents of R. Avraham's father, the Rambam. While he was one of the signers of the ban proclaimed in 1233 against some of the Rambam's writings, he later admitted to having been wrong in his actions against the Rambam. Rabbeinu Yonah speaks about practicing Hisbodedus within the chambers of one's spirit, within one's heart (*Sharei Teshuvah.* Shar 2:26. p 5168).

This is similar to the separation of wheat from chaff, selecting the useful, productive thoughts from the useless, worry-inducing doubts, in order to clearly focus on the real issues of life, on the Creator, and on one's purpose. Questions to ask are: Why am I here? What is my purpose? Where is my life heading? Am I living my full potential?

RABBI LEVI BEN GERSHON/
THE RALBAG

Intellectual Hisbodedus

Another very important medieval commentator and philosopher is Rabbi Levi Ben Gershon (1288 - 1344), known as the Ralbag or Gersonides to the world at large. He speaks of the subtle separation between states of consciousness for the purpose of entering a dream-like state for prophetic insight to occur.

The Ralbag describes two basic forms of intellect. There is the material, human intellect, which endows humans with the ability to learn and understand. And there is the Agent or Active Intellect, called *Seichel Ha'poel*, which survives death and contains all the wisdom and knowledge that we have acquired during our life through our *Seichel HaNikna*, "acquired intellect".

Our *Seichel*, "intellect", is rooted in *Seicehl Ha'Poel*, the "active or agent intellect", meaning the root of intelligence. Within our intellect itself there are various forms, e.g., *Seichel Yuli*, "potential intellect", *Dimyon*, "power of imagination", *Koach Nafshi HaMekabel*, "the power of spirit to receive", and so forth.

The Ralbag was interested in the question of why most intelligent and creative ideas come to us when we are in a waking state, whereas more prophetic, intuitive ideas are revealed to us in a dream-like state or while actually asleep (*Milchemes Hashem*, Maamor 2:5. p. 18a-18b).

The Ralbag reaches the understanding that while one is

asleep there is a separation between intelligence and imagination, of *Seichel* and *Dimyon*. Thus insights from the realm
of the unconventional, the ethereal or otherworldly can
be funneled down unobstructed and revealed. During the
waking state, however, there is a blurring of the faculties, so
that even when there is a revelation, the insight is muddled
and blurred (Ibid. p.19a).

The source of our intelligence is Seichel Ha'poel and the
ability to think comes from our *Seichel Yuli*, the "potential
of intelligence". Dreams, while they may be prophetic, in-
sightful, or intuitive are sourced in our Dimyon. Genuine prophecy comes from a higher source, where a person
works with his intelligence and simultaneously surrenders
other intellectual faculties causing a *Hisbodedus*, understood
as "isolation", between them and his *Koach Nafshi HaMekabel*, "the spirit power to receive", thereby receiving prophetic flow. Prophecy is a form of an emanation from the
Creator, using the medium of the Active Intellect first received by the Koach Nafshi HaMekabel, then assimilated
into the Dimyon and made clear in the rational facility of
the prophet.

All prophets prepared to enter into this meditative state,
inwardly separating their states of consciousness and then,
by Divine will, received an influx of prophecy. Moshe, on
the other hand, was able to surrender, at will, all of his other
intellectual faculties to his Koach Nafshi HaMekabel, call-

ing forth prophecy whenever he desired. In addition, when Moshe received Divine flow, his body did not tremble nor did it convulse in ecstasy, as was the involuntary reaction of all other prophets. For all of the other prophets, His-bodedus Penimi was a tension-filled task, an act of severing parts of self within, and expressing uncontrollable physical symptoms. The body experienced a breakdown, convulsing in a loss of self-control. The internal tension was expressed via the external tension of the body. Moshe, by contrast, was the master prophet able to easily separate with no conflict of internal and external. His body thus remained alert, upright and in control.

Years later, Rabbi Chayim Vital, the primary disciple of the Arizal, speaks of such a practice of separating levels within one's thoughts (*Shaarei Kedusha* 3. Shar 8).

The core of all of the above teachings, given over to us from R. Avraham, the Ralbag and the Maor Vashemesh, deal with clearing the mind so that it may become transparent and focusing the power of thought on what is truly desirable, opening up to deeper wisdom.

The practice we are going to delve into more deeply is called *Hashkata*, "silencing" or making quiet, coming from the root word *Sheket*, "silence". The core of the practice of Hashkata comes to us from over two thousand years ago, during the second half of the Temple period.

The Mishnah speaks of the practice of the early Chassidim saying, "The early Chassidm would wait one hour and then they prayed, so that their hearts (mind) can be directed to their Father in Heaven" (*Berachos*, 5:1). The language the Mishnah uses for "wait" שוהין is in transliteration spelled *Sho'in*, waiting, the act of being still.

The Rambam writes that they would settle their minds and quiet their thoughts, and only then commence to pray (*Pirush HaMishnayos*, Berachos 5:1). They would empty their minds before embarking on prayer.

The Mishnah quoted above begins, "One is not allowed to begin his prayers *Ela Metoch Koved Rosh*, "if not with due seriousness". Besides the simple meaning, as in seriousness, the words *Koved Rosh* could also mean "heaviness of the head", or a "cleaning and clearing of the head".

Before we begin to pray we too need to clean our minds and empty our hearts of all extraneous thoughts, feelings and sensations. Certainly we should not begin to pray when we are overwhelmed with feelings generated outside of the experience of prayer. Our sages tell us that we should not pray if we are feeling angry. (*Eiruvin* 65a. *Tur Orach Chayim*, Siman 98. See *Tosefos* ad loc. Today, the ruling is to pray either way. *Teshuvas Ha'gaonim. Sharei Teshuvah.* 89. *Mechaber.* Siman 98:2)

Before we embark on our path of prayer, we need to cleanse

our cluttered minds, quiet the noise and onrush of thoughts to welcome space for clarity. Making a cluttered mind more peaceful is one objective of *Sho'in*, the quieting of the mind. Whenever we wish to do any serious inner work we need to first ascertain that the mind is ready. Rabbi Bachya Ibn Pakudah, writes that when a person is engaged in duties of the heart, as for example prayer, he should first empty his heart from all distracting thoughts. (*Chovos Halevavos*, Shar Cheshbon Hanefesh 3;9. Note: *Sanhedrin* 22a. *Rambam*, Hilchos Tefilah 4;16. *Menoras HaMaor*, Ner 3. Klal 3;12, p. 306).

The Ran, Rabbeinu Nisan (on the Gemara ibid), however, writes that the Early Chassidim would *Sho'in* an hour before prayers. In that time, they would meditate on "the awesomeness of the Creator... and divest the mind and heart of all material pleasure" (*Ramah*, Orach Chayim, Siman 96). Not only would they empty and settle their minds, but they would also choose a particular thought to think about that summons up the awe of the Creator.

The objective is not to empty the mind of all thoughts, which, as will shortly be explored, is not (for the most part) attainable; rather, a quieting of one set of thoughts and introduction of another chosen set of thoughts.

This practice of the Early Chassidim was to empty their minds of all distracting thoughts, all mundane worries, and all random thoughts, and then to fill their minds with selected thoughts, thinking of the majesty or awesomeness of their Creator and connecting with their desire to get closer to G-d, and standing, as it were in the presence of the Creator.

These are some of the earlier sources that speak of quieting the mind, stilling the mind of the usual thoughts, and perhaps introducing more chosen, productive thoughts.

Let us now explore the method as was taught by the Rebbe, the master and teacher of Peasetzne.

RABBI KLUNIMUS KALMISH SCHAPIRO/ THE PEASETZNE REBBE

The Peasetzna Rebbe, Klunimus Kalmish Schapiro, was born in 1889 to Rebbe Elimelech, a noted Chassidic Rebbe who authored the *Imrei Elimelech*. He was named after his great grandfather, the *Maor V'shemesh*, R. Klunimus Kalmish Epshtein, a beloved Chassidic Rebbe, author and teacher.

While still a young boy, just two years of age, the Peasetzna Rebbe's father passed away. At the age of sixteen he married the daughter of R. Yechiel Moshe of Koznitz, the man who raised him from the time of his father's passing. In 1909, after the passing of his father-in-law, R. Klunimus Kalmish moved to Peasetzna and established his own Chassidic court. He and his wife had two children, a son and daughter, both of whom perished in the Holocaust.

After assuming the mantle of Rebbe his main focus was directed toward the education of children and young adults. In 1923, he established the Yeshivah "Da'as Moshe" in Warsaw where close to 300 students studied before the start of the war.

After the invasion of Poland, he was forced to live in the Warsaw Ghetto and continued, in secret, teaching, leading and inspiring those left remaining from the community. During this time, he also worked repairing shoes together with the *Rosh Yeshivah*, "head of the academy", of the famed school of Lublin. They would sit together for hours on end fixing shoes, tying the bottoms and tops together while immersed in words of Torah, holiness and purity. In this way, they unified the Upper and Lower worlds.

Although life in the Warsaw Ghetto was difficult beyond imagination, the Rebbe continued to inspire others, teaching Torah and offering comfort to those left bereaved. He also managed to write down weekly sermons that he gave to his students, dealing with issues such as faith in those troubling times, suffering, and the hidden face of Hashem. Eventually, the Rebbe realized that those surviving in the Ghetto were soon to be liquidated. He faithfully hid the pages of his manuscript, which he had written while in the

Ghetto, under a house. After the war, it was partially found and later published under the title, *Aish Kodesh*, the "Holy Fire".

Following the Warsaw Ghetto Uprising, one of the boys whom the Rebbe had nurtured back to health in his own home after a battle with typhus offered to save the Rebbe's life. He went to the Rebbe one night after the uprising and told him that through a passageway to an area the Nazis had secured as a safe zone, he could sneak out. The Rebbe responded with a "no", saying that he made a pact with 20 of his students and contemporaries that they would leave the Ghetto together only: "I go with all 20, or I stay and suffer along with their destiny." As it was not possible to rescue all pact members, the Rebbe remained in the Ghetto. A short time later, he was taken to a concentration camp near Lublin and then murdered by the Nazis in the fall of 1943 on the fourth day of the month of Cheshvan. May his holy memory be a source of blessing.

The uniqueness of the Peasetzne Rebbe was found in his primary focus on teaching young students, unlike most Chassidic Rebbe's who taught the older and more advanced students. His desire was to teach the youth the ways of Chassidic practice and its philosophical thought. He wished to convey to them the realness of G-d, how all of them, young as they may be, are able to experience true spiritual exaltation through a sense of closeness with their Creator.

A teacher to the youth and a very involved Rebbe, his teachings are both sincerely personal and simply practical. In his time, the day-to-day usefulness of Chassidic teachings was lacking, and the disciple was left to his own devices to discover how to bring such loftiness down into this realm. The Peasetzne went against the grain and taught practical application in partnership with the exalted Torah he gave over. He explained everything in the life of a Chassid or aspiring Chassid, including the ups and downs, the feelings of closeness and distance, the hopes and frustrations of a life of faith and spirituality. Through a very practical hands-on approach, the Rebbe guided his students along the path of spiritual advancement, both through his spoken teachings as well as those written in the pages of his manuscript.

HASHKATA — QUIETING THE MIND

A basic practice we have from the Peasetzne Rebbe is called *Hashkata*, "the quieting of the mind" from the onrush of unconscious thoughts.

The intention of *Hashkata* is not leading one toward *Ayin*, "nothingness", a mental state of total emptiness. Rather it is to quiet the mind, leading one to a more settled state free from the tyranny of distraction.

The notion of accessing Ayin is a fundamental teaching of the Maggid of Mezritch and his students, particularly

Reb Levi Yitzchak of Barditchav. In the Ayin practice, if it can be called a practice or doing, the idea is to reach Ayin, literally and simply to experientially be/feel (like) no-thing. Ayin is a state of total stillness, a place with no expression, what can be called "pure awareness", when we are not experiencing any thoughts or concepts. Sitting at the bank of the ocean and just feeling the waves wash up, coming up and down.

Experientially, the practice of Ayin, total stillness, is for the level of Tzadik, one who is without negativity, worry or uncertainty (*Tanya*, Chap 27). The Peasetzne points out numerous times in his writings that the goal of Ayin is, for most of us, unattainable. As his efforts were invested in educating the youth, who are more excitable and impressionable, the Hashkata practice is more readily accessible to all.

The Peasetzne Rebbe shares this story:

Once the students of the Baal Shem Tov heard that there was a great teacher that was passing through town, so they asked their master how will they know if indeed he is a great one or not? The Baal Shem Tov replied that this is simple to know. Ask the teacher if he has advice for how to rid oneself entirely of confusion-causing, negative thoughts. If he offers advice, know that he is false because there is no advice to rid oneself completely of negative thoughts. For it is man's destiny to struggle with extraneous thoughts, continually uplifting them until the time of death. (*Hachsharas Ha'Avreichim* . Chap. 3 p, 26. *Baal Shem Tov Al HaTorah*, Parshas Noach. Note 88)

People may think that by way of meditation they will clear their minds of the anarchy of noisy internal dialogue, but the mind is like a vacuum, always drawing in. For the purpose of energy efficiency, we can work to observe the thought process. In this witnessing, we will be able to notice how *meshuga*, "crazy" and erratic the nature of the mind is when left to its own devices. From here, we may open enough space to begin consciously feeding our minds with positive information.

In the words of the Peasetzne:

[excerpted and translated from, 'Derech HaMelech']

"Think about it, you can never stop and rest, thus, the mind thinks about one thing and flies to the next, from one similar thought to another similar thought, from there to another...thus to the mind all types of thoughts come in (when one does not have any control over his thoughts) even silly thoughts, even thoughts of doing negative actions..."

(Derech Hamelech, Vayeshev, 49).

The intended purpose of *Hashkata* is to regain some authority over our thoughts and quiet the inner static. We can never really concentrate on one topic or one image without the mind wandering into all different directions. Take a mundane issue, like thinking about your business. You decide you need to think about how your business is doing and you dedicate a few minutes to do so. But the moment you start thinking about your business your mind wanders into other areas, like what are you going to have for lunch. Hegemony is the aspired goal, to be able to gain some authority over one's thoughts and to quiet the inner static, controlling the randomness of thoughts. But how does one do so?

The Peasetzne speaks about this issue many times. What does one do when involved in prayer but the mind wanders to unrelated subjects? To this, he teaches:

[excerpted and translated from, 'Hachsharas Ha'avreichim']

"If with force you will try to get rid of these thoughts, I doubt you will be able to. And many times, these thoughts will overwhelm you even stronger (if you try to push them away). Therefore, stop your prayers for a period and relax yourself, calm down. If it is an appropriate time in prayer that you may sit down, sit down. If not, lean on something (simply relax yourself) and with a peaceful mind/heart observe your wild thoughts, how one thought leads to the next, jumping from one thing to the next..."

(Hachsharas Ha'avreichim, Chap. 9. p 128-129).

By observing your thoughts in a relaxed, non-forceful manner you will calm down your mind and increase your focus.

We will explore the practice of *Hashkata* in greater detail.

A student of the Peasetzne Rebbe wrote down the teaching below, which he heard firsthand from the Rebbe during the period of 1936-37:

[excerpted and translated from, 'Derech Hamelech]

"In the year 1936-37 I was called in to the Rebbe and that was the first time I heard about the idea of Hashkata. It is unfortunate what was forgotten, because I do not recall all the details, yet I have written what I do remember as a remembrance.

Our master, may his memory be a blessing, began with the teaching of our sages, 'A dream is one-sixtieth of prophecy' (Berachos, 57b). As it is known, the path of the master in his writings, that the Yeshus, "ego" and arrogance of a person is a hindrance for Hashra'ah, "Divine revelation" and awakening. Thus, if a person is awake, his mind and awareness is awake (i.e he is conscious of his ego and protective of self), it is thus difficult for a Hashra'ah from Heaven to rest upon him. However, when a person is asleep and his mind and thoughts are quiet, specifically then, since he has no self-awareness, it is possible that a Hashra'ah from Heaven will rest upon him. Thus, this is the reason why a dream is one-sixtieth of prophecy.

It also is a known teaching of our master, people are

more aroused in prayer than in study of Torah. Because in the study of Torah, one is more involved with the ego, i.e., 'I am learning, I am understanding'. However, in prayer it is the opposite — the main thing is nullification of the ego.

While asleep, it is impossible to want something as the ego is less pronounced, there is no longer the "I" to want or desire. Therefore, while in a waking state one can reach for a state of sleep, a quieting of thoughts and desires that overwhelm without end. The nature of thoughts is that one ties onto the next, making the process of extrication challenging. (As I have merited to hear from our master, if a person observes his flow of thoughts even for one day, he will see there is almost no difference between him and a crazy person, in terms of what they think about. The only difference is that the crazy person acts out his thoughts, whereas the sane, rational person lets his rational side make the decisions. But in terms of thoughts themselves, he is literally like a crazy person.) And he gave practical advice of how to quiet our thoughts.

He then spoke, saying that a person should begin by observing his thoughts for a few moments (around a few minutes), observing, 'What am I thinking about?'

By doing this observation he will start feeling that slowly, slowly his head is emptied and his thoughts stop from their regular relentless movement.

And then he should begin by saying one verse, e.g., 'Hashem our G-d is true', to connect his now empty mind from all other thought to one holy thought.

And afterwards, he can then ask for his needs, depending upon whatever attribute needs correcting (i.e. strengthening his faith, finding love, experiencing awe, etc.)

And I merited hearing from him the way to Hashkata is to strengthen faith.

And he said in his holy language: 'I believe with complete faith that the One Above is the only reality in the world. And there is no existence besides G-d in the entire world.

And everything that there is within the world is only a reflection of G-d.'

And one repeats this over and over again, but not saying this with strength (excitement) because the whole objective is to quiet the mind (the I, the ego), and when saying this with strength, he can arouse his I (ego). Rather, say the above statements in a genteel manner...

One can also practice Hashkata through Habatah, "observing", on the small hand of a clock, which barely moves.

Observing the slow movement of the small handle can also bring about Hashkata of his desires and thoughts.

After the Hashkata, which should bring about a type of Hashra'ah from Heaven, he (the Rebbe) said we should recite the verse, 'Hashem show me Your ways.' And say this verse with the special tune that he himself composed."

(Derech Hamelech, pp 450-451)

Now let us unpack this teaching and highlight the major points. A dream has prophetic possibilities, prophecy in terms of deeper insight into life and into oneself. The reason why prophetic insight is more accessible in sleep than in waking life is because in sleep the I, the ego, the conscious, aggressive self is quieted. Indeed the solution, suggests the Peasetzne Rebbe, is to create a dream-like state while awake, thus making room for *Hashra'ah*.

He calls this quiet, awake state *Hashkata*, in which the mind, the ego, the I — expressed within the internal dialogue which blocks the mind from receiving any form of *Hashra'ah* — is quieted. The normal thought patterns of *Yesh*, "ego", are subdued and one opens up to something beyond the ego.

When a person is consumed with thoughts of wanting, gaining, liking, or disliking, it is always the subjective i in the driver's seat leaving no space for something beyond the small self to penetrate and become revealed. In the language of our sages, regarding an arrogant person always thinking of the small self, they say, "I and him cannot rest in the same place', says Hashem" (*Sotah*, 5a). Indeed such a person is limited to thinking about the small i. We need to put aside the i in order to quiet the mind and experience something beyond ego.

The first and immediate objective is to quiet the mind, the ego, and then to experience something beyond ego. He also speaks of the value of this practice in terms of strengthening one's attributes, e.g., strengthening one's faith, love or awe of Hashem.

HASHKATA/ QUIETING THE MIND AND EGO

By quieting the normal egoic thought pattern, one can better establish his or her spiritual identity. Thinking of one holy thought in this quiet state and strengthening oneself to feel the *Kirvas Hashem*, the "closeness to Hashem", and experience a revelation of higher light from Above so as to be able to honestly say, "This is My G-d" (*Shemos*, 15:2).

When saying the classic blessing formula, *Baruch Ata Hashem...* "You are the Source of Blessing... the Master of the Universe," one should attempt to actually see with the mind's eye how the Creator, the King of the Universe, surrounds all of creation including you within it. See the entire world filled with Hashem's presence and feel yourself filled with that presence, as the Peasetzne writes (Hakdamah, *Bnei Machshava Tova*).

A person should not think: *Who am I? I know myself! I have done [such and such], how can I have such an experience to see the Divine presence filling the world?* "Do not despair," says the Peasetzne, "Because you are the child of prophets and you too can have a glimpse of the Infinite. And with this glimpse, this parting of the partition, the widening of your vision, the cleansing of your perception, you too can be up-lifted from the lusts of the body and become refined" (*Bnei Machshava Tova*, p. 32-33).

In another work, the Peasetzne instructs his students to know that they have a genetic spark of prophecy. "Israel, if they are not prophets, they are the children of prophets" (*Pesachim*, 66b). Inherently they have prophetic inspiration running through their blood. "Indeed," he says elsewhere, "they should lay claim and dig to reveal their inherent spark of prophecy within" (*Chovas HaTalmidim*, pp. 31-32).

The whole of Chassidus, according to the Peasetzne, is to walk in the ways of the prophets (*Hachsharas Avreichim*, Chap 1). As the Medrash says: "Heaven and earth is my witness, both a man or a woman, a Jew or a gentile, a slave or a maidservant, every person according to his or her action,

Ruach Ha'kodesh, "Holy Spirit" [a prophetic insight], will rest upon that person." And as the *Ye'aros Devash* writes, "It is known that every single one of us can attain awareness as the most chosen of prophets, until Moshe" (*Ye'aros Devash*, 1, Derush 11).

Hashkata is a requisite for deeper insights, more subtle awareness, or prophetic wisdom.

It is important to note that prophetic wisdom and insight does not predict the future, or direct you toward one particular action through a Heavenly voice. The prophecy that the Peasetzne speaks of is a form a prophecy available today, where a person has a different, deeper awareness. "Even though we no longer have prophecy…this is prophecy of predicting the future. However, prophecy of teaching a path and a revealing of Lights and Holiness certainly did not come to an end, Heaven forbid…So it appears, that any awakening of the heart resulting in an understanding and conception of holiness which arises within…is a form of prophecy and a revelation from Heaven" (*Derech HaMelech*, Shemos, p. 89).

The act of Hashkata is simultaneously a quieting of thoughts, as well as a quieting of the small self, thereby entering into a sleep-like state where there is less a pronounced and insatiable ego.

Interestingly, as mentioned in the Mishnah, "The Early Pious ones would *Sho'in*, 'wait', one hour and then they prayed". When turned inward, quieting down is not merely for the realm of the thoughts themselves, but also the whole structure of the tyrannical ego. The Early Pious ones would experience a *Hispashtus Ha'Gashmiyus*, a "divestment of materiality". This is a spiritual state wherein they were detached from bodily sensations, allowing them to meditatively enter into a state removed from physical form. They surrendered any psychic ties to the limitations of their physicality. This is a lofty stage analogous to a prophetic reality (*Tur*, Orach Chayim, 98. *Mechaber*, ibid. Shalah, *Asarah Hilulim*, p. 319. *Nefesh HaChayim*, Shar 2:14).

This divestment from the physical can be experienced via visualization of separation from one's body (*Sharei Kedusha*, 4), as well as even more so by internally silencing their *Yeshus*, "egoic sense of self". These Early Pious ones would, as R. Mendel of Vitebsk writes, empty and silence themselves of all outer physical sensations and experiences, and would attain a measure of divesting themselves of all materiality, ego and separate sense of I (*Pri Ha'aretz*, Vayakhel-Pekudie. See also: *Avodas Yisroel.* p 164. *Shearis Yisroel.* p. 3).

People walk around occupied with concerns various and sundry: *How can I get more honor? How can I make more money? What will I do tomorrow?* This challenges the inner Divine light, the spark of prophecy, making it harder to shine through the noise and veils of the ego. When the vessel is preoccupied with small i-ness in the form of doubt, fear, or worry, nothing can penetrate through. The inner-guided light — that part of self that gently moves one along his true path revealing the meaning and purpose of why he or she was created — is obscured. The inner light that illuminates what really matters and why we are here in the first place comes up against a roadblock.

Once in a while we are gifted with a splitting of the sea so to speak, a ceasing of the ego's constant cleaving to external forms and stimulus and in this moment the internal light can shine though crystal-clear. The Peasetzne Rebbe writes that on Yom Kippur, for example, a lot of people achieve major moments of clarity and lucidity, for indeed, on such a day, with all of its preparations and practices, the inner light shines through (*Bnei Machshava Tova*, p.11). Yom Kippur, is a period of time without food or drink when we remove ourselves completely, not just from pleasure, but also from even the possibility of physical pleasure. Thus we effectively remove ourselves from desire as well. It is a time without work, where we rest from our sense of identity as it is connected to our accomplishments. We cease defining ourselves by the job we have or the talents we possess. Yom Kippur is a time when we separate from physical relations, which normally provide us with a sense of self and self-worth. We thereby make space for our inner light to shine through unencumbered.

Detaching from these externally-oriented definitions of self, the veil of self is pulled aside and we can glimpse further down into the depths who we really are, even glimpsing our *Neshamah*, our soul, our purpose, our mission. Through the nullification of externally-defined identity, the inner essence is revealed.

Every moment can be a Yom Kippur-like moment; this opportunity is not merely reserved for once a year. If we choose to detach from the random gravity and addictive magnetism of distracting thoughts, our inner guiding light arises.

If one is totally preoccupied within the realm of the external, as the Peasetzne writes, nothing from within comes through. However, if one were to stop the thoughts that jump from one whim to the next, one's inner Divine spark would be revealed without any garments (*Derech HaMelech*, Bereishis, p. 5).

A DREAM STATE WHILE AWAKE

A dream state is another place where the inner Divine spark can be revealed as we are not preoccupied with our small i-ness.

There are four general brain wave types: Beta, Alpha, Theta and Delta. The Beta state is active when we are attentive and alert to external stimuli and when we exert mental effort. This Beta state is where we normally function from while awake. The Alpha state is active when we are awake, but relaxed. Theta is a state of daydreaming, fantasy, imagination, or inspirational thinking. Pure unconsciousness and deep, dreamless sleep are expressions of a Delta wave state. These four brain waves are varying frequencies of the electrical current that flows between parts of the brain in response or in conjunction with other brain and bodily activities. The frequency of Alpha, Beta, Delta and Theta is measured in cycles per second or Hertz (Hz). Light bulbs, for example, have a frequency of 60 Hz, which simply means that the filament flickers at a rate of 60 times per second, so fast that we perceive it as constant.

Our normal brain wave activity while in a waking state is Beta. This implies feeling rushed as time appears to pass by all too quickly. Beta is the fastest of brain wave activities with a frequency of 13 Hz.

We experience delta wave activity during sleep and restfulness. Delta is the slowest of brain waves with a frequency of 0 to 3 Hz.

Theta is a little faster with a frequency of 4 to 7 Hz and is most pronounced when we are falling asleep and waking up. During waking periods, this brain wave is associated with creative thinking or daydreaming.

Alpha activity is experienced during emotional equanimity and is a state in which blood pressure improves, as well as digestion and other regulatory functions of the body. With a frequency of 8 to 12 Hz. Alpha waves are associated with being alert, attentive and simultaneously relaxed.

For some years now, there has been a growing interest in the physical effects of meditation. Studies show that those who enter meditative states have a decrease in Theta and/or an increase in Alpha activity. A study was done on certain Rebbes entering states of Kavanah, similar to the state they would enter during prayer. The same results were yielded: Theta activity decreases, sometimes almost to nothing, while Alpha activity increases.

These effects are attainable by us as well. Through the Hashkata practice, the Beta activity is quieted and we enter into greater Theta and Delta states. Unlike the state of sleep, however, one remains conscious and able to choose their thoughts. This is an in- between state called hypnagogia, similar to the experience of the transitional states to and from sleep.

THREE STEPS TOWARDS HASHKATA:

STEP 1: *Habata* / OBSERVING

STEP 2: ONE VERSE FOCAL POINT

STEP 3: INTRODUCING A CHOSEN THOUGHT

STEP ONE

Habata:
OBSERVING THE RANDOMNESS OF THOUGHTS
TO QUIET THE MIND.

The objective is to quiet the mind, but how does one do this? The Peasetzne suggests that by simply observing one's thoughts, the act of observation will quiet the mind. This observing is called *Habata*. In his own words, "One should observe his thoughts for a few minutes, observing: *What am I thinking about?* By doing this observation, he will start feeling that slowly, slowly his head is gradually emptied and his thoughts stop from their relentless regular movement." In practicing *Habata*, the mindless rushing of thoughts from one to the other is slowed down.

As previously mentioned, the Chassidic masters living in Eastern Europe analogized the randomness of mind to "horse thoughts". That which is immediately in front of a horse is that which the horse focuses on. Put hay in front of a horse and they think hay; lead it to a steep road and it thinks steep road. The nature of the human mind can sadly work the same way. We walk down the street, hear a siren and think about a fire; notice a cloud and think about the weather. One random thought leads to another and yet another ad infinitum.

Even when a person consciously decides to be more focused and practice more controlled thinking, there is a challenge in achieving this. Notice the difficulty of concentrating for any extended period of time on a single subject. Extraneous thoughts interfere with your focus as if possessed by a mind of their own. As an experiment, resolve to focus your attention on a painting or a stationary object in front of you. How quickly does your mind begin to drift to other areas of the room? The mind easily burps up unrelated ideas to the matter at hand. It distracts and exhausts itself by straying and then needing to be reengaged. The Peastzne suggests that the overwhelming continuous chatter of the mind may be a sign of an insane person. The *Habata* quiets such chatter down.

In another text that the Peasetzne penned he writes that *Habata* is done with a critical mind, in order to observe the foolishness of one's own thoughts. He says that a person who is attempting to rectify his habit of entertaining negative, destructive thoughts should not linger in his mind.

[Excerpted and translated from 'Tzav V'Ziruz']

"And what is the advice for such a person who seeks a remedy, a complete remedy so that any negative thought should not ever live in his mind? For this there is not (no advice). However, the advice to weaken the craziness and to lessen the quantity of times these thoughts appear in his thoughts is lots of Habata. To continuously look at our thoughts... even if the first nine times we observe our (negative) thoughts we make the mistake thinking that these are beautiful and wise thoughts, the tenth time we will see correctly that they are nonsense, silliness, and we will be appalled by their craziness, and how such a thought could even find a place within our thoughts..."

(Tzav V'Ziruz, Chap 33. p. 360)

Here, *Habata* is used for the purpose of judgment. As we gradually become aware of the foolishness of such thoughts, we will no longer trust in them.

Additionally, the Peasetzne speaks here about *Habata* also in terms of looking at the slow movement of the small hand of a clock as a tool to slow down the internal dialogue. The purpose of this *Habata* practice is not for evaluation or judgment, but rather simple observation for the desired outcome of slowing down the mind. When we observe our thoughts, the mind begins to empty of them and grows toward stillness. Observation is the first step. Do not to fight with the thoughts that arise, or even judge them, just observe them and let them go.

Because the nature of the mind is to wander from thought to thought, we need the second step, a focal point, to hold our attention. The point of focus serves to steady our attention, allowing us to separate our awareness from any other intruding thoughts that arise like projections on a screen. As your attention is held to your focus, these thoughts fade.

STEP TWO

CHOOSE A WORD OR A VERSE AS A FOCAL POINT:

To help quiet the mind of horse thoughts, the Peasetzne suggests introducing a word, verse or phrase into your consciousness. A short teaching may also be chosen. This verbal focal point is then recited out loud so you are able to hear yourself speaking.

It is best to choose a word/verse/teaching that is familiar to you, so it will roll easily off your tongue and enter smooth into your ears, one that takes little or no effort to recall and repeat. Otherwise, it would be stress-inducing to remember and therefore, counter-productive along the path toward Hashkata.

This audible repetition serves as a reference point of return for you. Observing and noticing your thoughts, and simultaneously holding your awareness on this one thought, allows your mind to eventually fill with this and this only. For this reason it is important to select this phrase carefully.

Whenever the mind wanders astray, we observe this detour through *Habata,* and with the help of our chosen saying we gently guide the attention back to center.

In order to gain hegemony over our thoughts and be the owners of that which circulates in our minds, rather than being owned by it, we start small, reducing the chance of hyper- extension or over-stimulation.

Many of the early Chassidic Rebbes speak about entertaining one thought at a time to keep the mind steady (*Ohr Ha-Ganuz,* Likutie Baal Shem Tov, 86). This is like a default thought. A person should always have one small default thought that can be summoned to the forefront of the mind without hardship or struggle.

Reb Mendel of Premishlan, a student of the Baal Shem Tov taught, "You should always have only one thought in the service of Hashem…because when a person has many thoughts he becomes confused. This one thought," says Reb Mendel, "is that everything there is in this world is all filled with the Creator" (*Hanhagas Tzadikim* 1. p 238).

This teaching has far-reaching ramifications. The basic idea is that we should have this one profound thought — that everything is from Hashem — so that no matter what happens, it is all good (at least, it is all for the good). The more far-reaching implication is that many times people who want to grow or change patterns of their behavior are not simple or specific enough to be effective. For instance, a person says, "I would like to be a better father/mother." This is a very broad and general statement. Instead, the Chassidic masters say, *take one thought, nothing fancy, just one simple thought*, and work from there. For instance, "Every time my child comes home from school, I will give him/her ten minutes of my time." One small thought is worth more than many grand thoughts. One thought, one idea, one movement is all we have. Every marathon begins with one step — every journey, with just one movement.

Summarizing the second step: If you want to quiet down the mind, simply observe your thoughts. Then introduce one small, easy thought and recite it over and over again. It is very important that this thought, word, verse or phrase that you choose as your audible focal point be something that you have no difficulty remembering. Otherwise, you will build up stress in the process. This would be counterproductive to our objective. If you experience difficulty remembering your focal point because it does not feel authentic or is too complicated and wordy, agitation will grow and you will become ever less settled.

This thought, word, verse or phrase you choose will be your focal point and will hold your attention. When you sense some inner quiet and you feel more mentally and emotionally settled, you can then enter step three, which is to intentionally introduce an issue or larger idea, a more expansive thought that needs clarity. The only way to experience clarity of mind is to first quiet the mind of pervasive thought junk by practicing *Hashkata*.

STEP THREE

INTRODUCING A CHOSEN THOUGHT:

Once the mind is quiet and calm, focus is tangibly accessible. You are now at the right place to introduce a more elaborate thought or issue that needs resolution, such as a particular trait that needs strengthening or overcoming.

There are many issues in life that demand our mindfulness and attention. They can be certain decisions we need to make or certain areas in our emotional or spiritual development that need tending to. Often, the moment we decide to start thinking about these pertinent issues, the mind exhibits having a mind of its own, introducing a whole slew of other thoughts, haphazardly rushing from one to the next.

Now that the mind is quieter and our focus more alert,

the opportunity has arrived to take advantage of this still-ness and introduce an issue that is pressing. Whether it is a question that is nagging you or a choice you need to make which is shrouded in uncertainty.

This is the time to properly open up, without distraction, in order to find a resolution to the query or to receive clarity in the midst of uncertainty.

In review:

You have observed your thoughts, allowing them to run around and tire themselves out like children at recess run-ning every which way. You have introduced your focal point, the word or short verse/phrase you have chosen to repeat to yourself over and over again. This focal point must be easy to remember and light to exit the mouth. As you observe the thoughts coming and going, loyally return to your focal point, to your center. Once you feel settled via *Habata*, now introduce the larger idea from which you are seeking reso-lution or the practical affirmation that you want to integrate into your life.

You are now ready to think with a clear, settled mind.

A NIGUN/ MELODY

After this practice of *Hashkata*, which may also bring about *Hashra'ah*, some form of clarity or insight into yourself or purpose, the Peasetzne says that one should conclude with a tune. He suggests singing a *Nigun*, a soothing "wordless melody".

Music in general, and a Nigun in particular, has the power to soothe. If the listener or singer is nervous, tense or disconcerted, the music has the ability to transform the negative state to one of inner tranquility.

Traditionally, a Nigun contains no beginning or end and it is sung over and over again. The word Nigun, when written in Hebrew, is a palindrome: Nun- Gimel- Nun. As such, it is truly endless. Its direction is inward and its flow is soothing, rather than outward and erratic. The tunes are progression-oriented, desiring to take the listener on a journey from point A to point B. Their point of departure is clear, their middle is strong, and their ending, definitive.

The Nigun's intention is the endless journey inwards. Every note of the Nigun can be a beginning and when one reaches its end, a new beginning has arrived.

A repetitious melody or rhythm has a very soothing nature. Our sages in the Talmud speak of the sound of continuously dripping water upon a hard surface, drip drop drip drop, as helping a person fall asleep, which is a state of over-relaxation (*Eiruvin*, 104a. *Shulchan Aruch* Orach Chayim, 338. *Magen Avraham*. 1). Similarly, sitting next to a stream of rushing water works as a soothing agent. The sound of the water can calm a person's nerves and bring them greater ease.

Music has the wonderful ability to calm nerves and to lessen anxiety (*Berachos*, 57b. *Maharsha*, Shelosha Moshivim, ad loc. *Safer Hamevakesh*. R. Shem Tov Falaquera (1970) p. 12). Overall, music cures shattered nerves (*Samuel 1* 17. *Radak*. Ad loc. *Rambam, Shemonah Perakim*. Chap. 5. R. Moshe Yechiel of Levertov. *Safer Shemiras HaDa'as, Aimrei Tal. Ma'amar Nigun*. pp 5 - 7.) Ending the meditation with a *Nigun* befits *Hashkata*, which in itself is a practice of calming the mind and heart.

Our sages teach that an omen for success in study is to be in close proximity to a stream of water (*Kerisus*, 6a. *Horios*, 12a). The continuous sound from the rushing water serves as a type of natural Nigun. At first, the relaxing sound of the water fills the mind, while simultaneously emptying it from all distracting thoughts, allowing the mind to be more empty and at ease, allowing one to meditate with more clarity.

In addition to the sound of the Nigun as a relaxing agent there is another purpose, and that is that through the Nigun, the idea of focus — first simple, then more expanded — can be more easily digested. The sound helps the mind relax into a state of *Hashkata*, allowing us to enter a meditative state of stillness.

This idea works with any type of Nigun, even a very simple tune. There is something physiological to this. Sustained, internally-generated rhythm and vibration can help relax the body and, in turn, the mind; much like how the ebb and flow of the ocean and the pulse of the wind can soothe our splintered psyches, even to the point of putting us to sleep. Which is actually one of the hidden points of this form of meditation — to surrender ourselves to something which resembles a state of sleep all the while remaining awake and alert, like a lucid dream. This allows us behind-the-scenes access to parts of ourselves usually off-limits when in a normal waking state of self-conscious awareness, where our default mode is generally defensive. When we meditate, we are able to relax our default mode and choose a different setting altogether, closer to objective response rather than knee-jerk reaction.

One may choose to add words to the Nigun that are consistent with their one thought which they introduced into their calm mind, or even take the one thought or thoughts and putting them to a tune. This allows the words and their meanings and applications to enter into consciousness via a path of non-force. As will be explored in the teachings of R. Yisrael of Salant, this is the desired result of the *Hashkata* practice: To calm the mind, introduce a simple focus, and then expand on it without stirring up any exertion.

Nigun helps the clarified message to enter more deeply into our psyche in a non-coercive manner. And if we add words, it has the possibility of seeping into one's subconscious, without overload or stress, just gently sliding into the deeper recesses of the brain and lodging there, reworking the hardwire of the brain.

The idea of ending with a Nigun is also connected to other teachings by the Peasetzne in which he speaks of a Nigun's power to reveal the essence of the soul (*Bnei Machshava Tovah*, Os 18, 42-43). The Nigun helps reveal this potential as it also triggers a *Hashra'ah*, a revelatory awakening.

A favorite spiritual practice among all groups of Chassidim is to sit together and sing Nigunim. "Speech is the pen of the heart", says the master of Mussar, Rabbi Bachya Ibn Pakudah (*Chovos Halevavos*. Shar Habechinah. 5). The Alter Rebbe adds, "Song is the pen of the soul" (*Sefer Hasichos 5402*, p. 122). A Nigun is the expression of the inner depths of the singer's heart and soul.

Such is the power of a Nigun — to awaken us to something deeper within by way of relaxing the rational, active left brain and allowing a deeper premonition, insight, or intuitive wisdom to emanate and permeate from the right brain.

An additional point about music in general, and Nigun in particular, is that music has the power to create a certain divestment from the physical. When the ancient Israelite prophets would seek to enter into prophetic states of consciousness they would summon musicians to play so they could hear the "sweetness of the sound of the music"; for through such music, "they (the prophets) would enter into a state of internal isolation (divesting from the coarse body) and their spirit would separate — meaning goes out into the music" (R. Chayim Vital, *Sha'arei Kedusha*, 4:2). Music isolates the internal mind from its external clutter until one is able to completely immerse oneself within it, merging all of one's faculties with the Heavenly melody. For this reason, the prophets would use music as a tool to separate their consciousness from mundane reality and focus solely on the Divine (*HaMaspik L'Ovdei Hashem*, Erech Hisbodedus). There is a peculiar nature to sound in that it unbinds the brain from the rest of the being. Snap your finger around the circumference of your head, at ear level, and it will feel this detachment.

The Peasetzne Rebbe lays down for us the path for *Hashkata* with the explicit intention of enhancing our spiritual development with expert guidance.

We will now introduce a practical how-to guide for you to perform this profound practice of Hashkata.

MEDITATION I

HASHKATA & HABATA

....

QUIETING THE MIND & OBSERVING

....

EMPTYING THE MIND OF EVERYDAY THOUGHTS
BY OBSERVING THEM, INTENTIONALLY RELEASING THEM
AND THEN BRINGING THE MIND TO FOCUS
WITH A CHOSEN THOUGHT.

MEDITATION BEGINS WITH THE COMMITMENT TO SHOW UP to this present moment. Expectations of how the experience should be for you are to be put aside. It is preferable to carve out a time that can be fully allocated to your meditation practice, free from other commitments and distractions. Clear a space that is welcoming, clean and comfortable for you to sit for a set amount of time. Regarding the duration of how long to sit for, it is suggested to start out small and stay consistent, rather than aim high and eventually feel overwhelmed and unmotivated to continue.

Meditation is a practice of being present, of showing up and honoring that nothing else need be done in this moment, so set up your meditation time in such a way that you can be fully available to it. It might mean waking up a few minutes early, before everyone else's day begins and your responsibilities to others ensue or maybe, for you, it means taking a proper break away from the computer. Treat yourself to this experience of needing to do nothing else but be where you are.

HABATA/HASHKATA MEDITATION

STEP BY STEP:

Before you begin, choose a word or a verse to serve as an audible focal point to calm and center you. (e.g. All is One, Create for me a Pure Heart, All existence is a reflection of The Divine). In addition, choose a question or a character trait that challenges you and you wish to resolve.

Turn off your ringer. Sit in your designated meditation spot comfortably and relaxed, but not overly relaxed that you may fall asleep. Take a few shoulder rolls and stretches raising your arms over your head and releasing them with the breath to relax your upper body and stretch your lung tissue for easy, natural breathing.

Set a soft timer in order to fully enter this meditation without any worry of what needs to be done afterwards. This time is for being present. Allow yourself the gift of this experience. For those new to meditation practice, it is recommended to start anywhere from 10-20 minutes. This is not a competitive practice so best to start small and slowly, steadily build on a strong foundation.

Invite all of yourself into this space here and now. You do not need to close your eyes, but it may be helpful.

Hashkata/ Quieting the mind: As you sit in this safe space of silence and solitude, various sounds, sensations, thoughts and feelings may arise. Allow them to surface without the need to hold onto, internalize or judge them. As they come, so they go. Is there noise coming from outside? Do you feel an urge to reach for your phone or your to-do list? Is it secretly enjoyable to know that there is nothing else you need to do in this moment other than be here now? Take a few deep breaths of transition. With each exhale, let it all go and simply be.

Habata/ Observation: Gently bring your aware- ness to your thoughts. Are they random? Foolish? Incessant?

As you practice Habata, softly recite your chosen saying again and again. Let this serve as the focal point of your meditation, returning your mind to center when it wanders off. The repetition of this saying diffuses distraction.

With gentle awareness, you may sense that your head is becoming more empty and quiet. If your mind wanders astray, return to your focal point.

Keep on reciting over and over again your chosen saying. Do so with gentleness and calm. Try not to work yourself up.

As the mind reaches quiet and settled shores, introduce your question, challenge or affirmation. Now is the time for the bigger issue you are dealing with to enter. Allow this challenge or the affirmation to be your new saying, repeating it smoothly and steadily, again and again.

Sit with it and become open to an inner awakening and clarity.

When the timer goes off, do not run off with the urge to rush back into a fast, thoughtless pace. Seal your meditation with a prayer in a Nigun/ song that everything you have just worked is being realized. Seal your meditation with an offering of gratitude.

MEDITATION II

QUIETING THE MIND

For Every Day Living

PRACTICAL DAILY APPLICATION

THIS TEACHING FROM R. AVRAHAM, THE SON OF THE Rambam, similar to the teachings of the Peasetzne Rebbe, is centered on ethics and spirituality. By focusing thought, first something simple then something more complex ultimately leading to inner spiritual awakening. As the ability to quiet the onrush of thoughts is always beneficial, the core idea of learning how to quiet the mind through Habata/ observation is applicable in many of life's situations.

The Peasetzne speaks of the spiritual developments in terms of *Avodas Hashem*, divine service, but his teaching, the way of Habata and Hashkata and the way to quiet the mind and then introduce a question, an issue on hand, can work with every issue of life.

The practice of Hashkata teaches us how to gain control over our inner selves, to be become less anxious, more focused and less overwhelmed by unrelated horse thoughts. It is, therefore, valuable both spiritually and practically.

Simple observation of thoughts serves to calm us. Using an audible focal point to quiet our minds and introducing a question that needs to be resolved. In this quietness, practiced with as little efforting as possible, we are able to think more clearly and hold focus more easily.

HASHKATA CAN BE VERY HELPFUL IN MANY of life's decisions, both big and small, is this the right person for me, or should I take this job. In situations where we find ourselves having a hard time reaching clarity, feeling stuck and overwhelmed in indecision, this practice is applicable. While we often know, on a very deep level, the answers to our questions, the deluge of incoming thoughts and emotions invites uncertainty. By way of cleansing our vessel, uncluttering the mind and settling our emotions, we invite objective clarity to rise.

Once we quiet the mind through Habata, the mind then has space to ponder our most pressing questions and concerns. Once the mind is quieter and the emotions are checked, we can think more objectively and clearly.

Whether seemingly big or small, trivial or profound, this method of meditation is meant to deliver. Often, when seeking resolution to an issue at hand, a deluge of unrelated ideas enter your mind and hinder the thought process or you feel scattered, mind jumping from one idea to the next in a random, almost frantic way. Hashkata alleviates these symptoms.

The idea is to slowly train yourself to think clearly. First, through Habata you try to slow down the onrush of unrelated thoughts and sensations, you begin to observe your thoughts objectively, as if on a screen, without arousing emotions. You continually keep chanting a small verbal focal point to anchor yourself, and to have an inner place to return to. Once you feel that the mind and emotions are somewhat settled, quieted, you introduce the issue that is troubling you, or the question you have, or the affirmation you desire to become.

These are very incremental steps. Slowly from one small chosen thought, your focal point, you can introduce more intricate and detailed thoughts, and keep a clear, uncluttered, non-scattered mind thought-out. This is the beauty of this simple yet profound practice.

Here is a practice outline and guide, to the practice of Hashkata, the quieting of the mind for any issue on hand.

MEDITATION II:
QUIETING THE MIND
For Every Day Living

STEP BY STEP:

Everyone has an optimal time for practicing meditation. While it is great to develop consistency in your practice, this exercise is beneficial at any juncture throughout the day. Whether you are dealing with a lack of focus, indecision or anxiety, take a few moments to practice the quieting of the mind.

Prior to beginning, place the question you are working on in the front of your mind.

Sit in your designated meditation spot comfortably and relaxed, but not overly relaxed that you may fall asleep. Closing your eyes gently is recommended.

Take a moment for letting go of all the internal noise, chaos and fluctuations. Simply be.

You may notice various sounds, bodily sensations, thoughts or feelings arise. Without manipulating or changing a thing, observe it all.

Choose a sound, word or saying that is easy for you to repeat as your focal point.

Gently anchor your awareness in this focal point, repeating it steadily and smoothly over and over again.

Begin the practice of Habata: Observe your thoughts with gentleness and calmness. Do not judge them or get upset with yourself for having such thoughts. Allow yourself to simply observe and let go, returning to your focal point.

Repeat to yourself, over and over again, a sound, word or words, and keep going back to this sound. Many thoughts come up, observe, and go back to the focal point.

As the mind is settles and the onrush of random thoughts quiets, introduce your more complex question.

Slowly and softly, repeat the question to yourself over and over.

As you approach the issue from a place of steady calm, you invite resolution to rise. Allow it to settle and sit with it.

. . . .

Seal your practice with a prayer of hope and longing for the answer you receive to be actualized and integrated into your life.

. . . .

Gently open your eyes.

. . . .

MEDITATION III

OBSERVING ONE'S THOUGHTS

THE FIRST STEP IN THE HASHKATA METHOD OF
meditation and self-observation is Habata, the observing of
ones thought patterns. The objective is to quiet the mind
of the deluge of unwanted and intruding thoughts. There
is also a method that teaches by casually and objectively
observing one's thoughts, without obsession or indulgence,
a person will truly understand what areas of his life need
special attention and repair.

Our stream of consciousness teaches us much about ourselves. If the mind continually wanders, we can observe to
where it goes. The mind tends to wander to the areas of our
lives which we cling to or are bound by. As it would appear
most sensible to release the grip of these concerns as they
hamper our ability to focus, by bringing a non-judgmental
awareness to them, we will be able to follow the concern to
its root and begin the work of repair.

If in the midst of prayer, study or any other activity that demands focused attention, and our mind independently goes
off-track, the first step is to pause and let the thought drift
away. Superficial thoughts will dissolve. But what happens
if this particular thought keeps on popping up, not matter
how hard we struggle to let go? This reveals the thought
to be deep in our psyche. Reoccurring thoughts are simply
demands for inner work.

For the purpose of self –evaluation it may be a good idea to take a gentle short glance at your thoughts, so long as they are not detrimental. By simply noticing what grabs your imagination and fills your thoughts, you will know where you are holding in life and what demands to be repaired.

Honesty is integral. We need to be honest with ourselves in order to admit what stage of consciousness we are holding, regardless of how unflattering it may be. As we observe rather than reject our inner world, we are empowered to go deep within and refine. From there, we embrace our authenticity and open to living our greatness.

MEDITATION III:

OBSERVING ONE'S THOUGHTS

....

STEP BY STEP:

....

The familiarity of this exercise is found in our tendency to practice it without effort or awareness on a regular basis. As you bring more intention to your meditation practice, your experience of observing will refine your clarity and shine light on areas in your life that are calling out for improvement.

....

Apply your attention to the title of this chapter, letting it serve as your focal point. You are invited to close your eyes and create a visual to accompany these words. As you enter this space of clear intention, your mind will wonder, within a matter of minutes or moments, elsewhere. Pause for a moment, allowing the intruding thoughts to vanish as easily as they arose and return your focus. If a particular distracting thought persists, continue with this practice.

....

Sit in your designated meditation spot comfortably, but not overly relaxed that you may fall asleep. Closing your eyes is recommended.

....

Bring to your mind's eye the title of this chapter which serves as your focal point.

Various sounds, sensations, thoughts or feelings may begin to cross your mind. Allow for these distractions without any effort to alter or understand them. Hold your center.

Returning to your focal point and welcome in fresh ideas on observation.

As your focus steadies, open to the awareness of where your mind wanders. Observe with gentleness and objectivity, not entering deeply into the deluge of emotions or judgments that tempt to overshadow. Resisting distraction only serves to empower distraction. Whether these thoughts are of someone to whom you hold a grudge, or a debt you want to pay off, or a new hobby you want to explore, watch them from your grounded seat.

While maintaining focus on your focal point, simultaneously observe where your mind wanders, but do so without actually 'going there.' Simply, notice and observe.

Make a resolution to work on this area in your life that keeps on coming up. Verbally declare: I am going to deal with [such and such] issue.

. . . .

Let this experience settle, let the greater awareness of yourself seep in. Seal your practice with gratitude for the opportunity to self-work from a place of love.

. . . .

PART TWO

BREATH

PART TWO

BREATH

BREATH: THE ESSENCE OF LIFE

OFTEN, WHAT IS MOST SIMPLE IS WHAT IS MOST profound. That which we take for granted is the most essential; that which is right in front of us is the most important.

The sages of old have debated about just what the most essential ingredient in life is: food, clothing, shelter? An even deeper line of questioning is: How can we recognize what in life is that which we really need? What is excess? And what causes us more pain and worry than good?

Rabbi Bachya Ibn Pakudah, the famed 11th century moralist and philosopher, poses the question: What is the most essential ingredient for life? Maimonides, the Rambam, answers in his Guide for the Perplexed: That which is the cheapest and most available is that which is the most essential. The more obtainable something is, the more we actually need it.

Shelter costs more than clothing, proof that clothing is more essential to our well-being than shelter. Food in general, and staple foods like bread in particular, is cheaper than clothing, thus bread is more essential. Water is even cheaper than bread, thus water is the more essential of the two. Cheapest of them all is air, which is free. Air allows us to breathe, and breathing is vital for our existence.

We can exist, albeit with difficulty, without shelter, we can live without bread, and we can go at least a few days without water. We cannot exist for more than a few minutes without oxygen.

Breathing is so natural, so automatic, and yet a simple awareness of the metaphoric value of breath can transform an often unconscious and automatic experience into a profound form of meditation and intentional living.

The process of simple, conscious breathing can teach us more about ourselves, about life, and about the Divine creative process than all of the intellectual philosophies.

THE ABOVE IN THE BELOW,
THE SIMPLE AS THE PROFOUND

Among the illustrious teachers and transmitters of Kabbalah, the inner dimension of Torah, there is one great who stands out as the embodiment of the principle that often the most simple is the most profound. He is the early 18th century mystic, Rabbi Yisrael ben Eliezer, the Baal Shem Tov.

With the teaching of the Baal Shem Tov, all the theoretical and cosmological teachings of Kabbalah were applied to the individual's psycho-spiritual development and personal experience. The path of the Baal Shem is to turn everything inwards toward the soul, to apply each lesson in an individual way, and to constantly be reaching towards the Infinite Beyond.

The earlier Kabbalists and mystics spoke of the higher Lights above. The Baal Shem Tov came along and explained how all these Upper lights are reflected in this world below and within the human being.

The novice who has only glimpsed theoretical Kabbalah, tends to view these teachings and stories as a writing replete with fantasy, strange happenings, mythical landscapes, and

a seemingly irrational and unrealistic worldview, completely unrelated to reality. The following parable is related by a
famed Kabalistic and Chassidic Master, the Tzadik of Zit-
dotshav.

*In a time when travel was a perilous and arduous venture
and most people had never been outside their little village, a
man journeyed to a distant land. Upon his return, he gathered together the people of his village and enthusiastically
related the great adventures of his voyage. He spoke of a bird
he had seen in a distant land, whose features were remark-
able. For example, the bird's face was human, his eyes were
the sun, and his legs were that of a giraffe's. The villagers
scoffed and dismissed his story as utter fantasy.*

*But there was one fellow villager who was positively in-
spired by the adventurers of his tales, and he set out on the
same voyage determined to see the world for himself. Years
later he returned to his village, a man of the world. Like the
traveler who had so inspired him, he gathered the village
folk and related his adventures. He too spoke of this fantastic
bird, but the description was slightly different. The face of
the bird, he said, was not actually human, although it did
bear close resemblance. The eyes were bright, but not actually the sun, and the legs were long and spindly bringing
to mind the giraffe, however, they were most certainly not
actual giraffe's legs. Upon hearing this man's story, the villagers were divided. Some wholeheartedly believed this man*

whose story was more convincing than the first traveler's. Yet there were plenty of skeptics to whom the story sounded entirely contrived.

One of the villagers was determined to bring a final conclusion to the matter of this strange bird and undertook the arduous journey himself. Upon his return he gathered together the villagers and triumphantly proclaimed: The matter is settled! Whereupon, he reached into his large bag and withdrew the strange and fantastic bird. This time there was not a skeptic to be found.

This parable relates to the stages in the revelation of the inner secrets of Torah over the course of the last thousand years. First, the Zohar, which contains the teachings of the 1st century Rabbi Shimon Bar Yochai, was revealed in the 13th century. The Zohar describes the Divine presence and our relationship with the *Ein Sof*, "Infinite Light". In the Zohar, we find such strange and fantastic tales, such mythical and mystical configurations that we can hardly believe. In the 16th century, in Safed, the city of mystics, the Kabbalah began to take on a more comprehensive and analytical form. Patterns and systematic thought processes began to appear in Kabalistic literature. The main facilitator and preeminent teacher was R. Yitzchak (Isaac) Luria, the holy AriZal. Centuries later, the Baal Shem Tov founded the mystical movement known as Chassidism. With the birth of the Chassidic movement, Kabbalah came to its full fruition. The Baal Shem Tov brought the image of the Creator into reality. No longer were these mystical concepts far-fetched and unrealistic. They became a concrete part of our everyday lives, affecting every facet of creation. Heaven was brought down to Earth.

Merging heaven and earth, the Baal Shem Tov was a master of apparent paradox, proving how the bird of the parable actually lives among us. The Baal Shem Tov revealed how the simple is utterly profound.

The Baal Shem and his disciples spoke of various practices of meditation and intention which all emphasized simplicity. Let us first begin to get acquainted with who the Baal Shem Tov was in order to better understand the novelty of his teachings.

WHO WAS THE BAAL SHEM TOV?

Baal Shem Tov means the "Master of the Good (Divine) Name". His actual name was Yisrael, "Israel". He was born in 1698 in Okop, a small village in the Ukraine on the Polish-Russian border. His parents, Eliezer and Sarah, were quite old when he was born and they both passed away when he was a still a very young boy. Before leaving this world, his father called over little Yisrael and said to him, "Have no fear. Fear nothing other than the Creator."

His early life is shrouded in mystery. But we do know that the young orphan was cared for by the community. During his youth, perhaps lacking shelter to call home, he found solace wandering alone in the fields and forests. He would spend hours on end surrounded by nature, pouring out his heart to the Creator in great love and awe. Being alone, he came to realize that man is never alone, and that Hashem, the Creator is always present.

As a teenager, he supported himself as a teacher's assistant. Later on in life, he showed a fascination with the Hebrew Aleph Beis and drew great mystical insight and spiritual inspiration from the simple sounds and shapes of the letters, as we will touch upon later. This too can be traced to his years spent with children learning with excitement, for the first time, the sacred letters of the Aleph Beis.

Throughout his younger years, although spiritually evolving and developing as a great mystic, Kabbalist and healer of the body and soul, the Baal Shem Tov maintained an image of simplicity — he dressed, walked and talked like the average man of the village.

Legend has it that during this formative period in his life he developed a close relationship with other *Nistarim*, "hidden Tzadikim", a secret society of Kabbalists; and most importantly with Rabbi Adam Baal Shem, who would become his teacher.

When Yisrael was thirty-six years old, he received a message from Heaven to reveal himself to the world. In a short period of time, his fame as a holy man grew swiftly and he became known as Yisrael Baal Shem Tov. The title Baal Shem was a name given to many holy men who were miracle workers, as his teacher was known as, Adam Baal Shem. Settled in the small town of Medzeboz in Western Ukraine, and supported by the community as the local Kabbalist, many noted scholars became the Baal Shem's disciples. The foundation of the Chassidic movement was established and would flourish after his passing in the spring of 1760.

The Baal Shem Tov himself did not write down his teachings. What he did leave us with are his disciples — living, breathing examples who embody his teachings. These living books eventually wrote down some of the teachings of their master and it is from them that we get a glimpse into this great, revolutionary, profound yet simple master. As the Baal Shem spoke in Yiddish and his books were written in Hebrew, one needs a fine tuned eye to discern when perhaps a nuance was lost in translation.

UPSIDE DOWN- INSIDE OUT

This is a synopsis of his life, although the Baal Shem Tov is a much larger-than-life figure. He inspired a real revolution, turning the heavens upside down, where the Above becomes revealed in the below, and inside out, where the inner spiritual reality becomes manifest in the exterior shell of material reality.

All of the core teachings of Torah and Kabbalah became accessible through the Baal Shem Tov. He made it possible for mundane activities, such as eating and sleeping for example, to become opportunities for Yichudim, "unifications", thereby transforming a mundane act into a sacred act.

A Yichud is a spiritual intention and meditation to connect heaven and earth. For the AriZal, the practice of Yichud was done when a person wraps Tefillin, or waves Lulav and Esrog. For the Baal Shem Tov, a Yichud can be done when eating a meal or chatting with a friend in the street.

GENERAL SOUL

There are those of us who possess a *Neshamah Kelalis*, a "general soul", and there are those who possess a *Neshamah Peratis*, a "specific soul". A person with a specific soul-type is someone that is one-dimensional. There are *tzadikim*, "spiritual giants", who attain *Tzidkus*, "greatness in one area of life", but are lacking in other areas. For instance they may be great scholars, who sit and learn the whole day, but they do not pray with the deepest *kavanah* - meaning, their intellectual acumen is sharp and focused, but their devotional life is flat and uninspired. There are others who are not very learned, but they reach great heights through prayer. And there are those who neither have scholarship, nor do they pray, but are very loving people with open hearts and open homes. These are all great people with a Neshamah Peratis. A general soul is all encompassing. Such a person studies, prays, loves, and excels on all dimensions of being human. The Baal Shem Tov is one such Tzadik. There are many stories that express this. His love for others is legendary, his prayers were profound, and amongst his students were renowned scholars in their own right, such as the Maggid of Mezritch, who was formally a student of the famed Pnei Yehoshuah, and Reb Yaakov Yoseph of Polonnye. They all attest to their teacher's extraordinary Torah knowledge, creativity and wisdom.

Being a general soul, his teachings involve all of life. There are teachings of the Baal Shem Tov on the path of art, song, music and dance, as well as silence. There are teachings of the Baal Shem Tov about how to eat and celebrate, and teachings that speak of how to refrain and restrain. The Baal Shem Tov's teachings encompass all of life, the ups and the downs, the noise and the silence, the joy and the sadness, the movement and in stillness.

TWO MODALITIES OF ECSTASY

Let us begin by reading some diverse and even seemingly paradoxical teachings. In one, the Baal Shem Tov speaks about experiencing Deveikus in a quiet voice.

[Excerpted and Translated from the 'Tziva'as Harivash']

"A person has to accustom himself to pray, even the songs of prayer, with a low, genteel voice, and to scream in silence...A cry, a scream that comes from a place of Deveikus is silent."

(Tziva'as Harivash, 33. p. 5b)

In this inner state of stillness, of genuine Deveikus, one's prayers become more inwardly directed and quieter, resounding within a certain stillness. A cry from a place of Deveikus is low, with no displayed emotions and with no or very little body movement.

When one senses oneself outside the Unity of the Creator, in order to re/connect with the Source, there needs to be an outward expression. For from this place, a person is seeking to connect with something outside of themselves; as they are separate, or feel themselves to be separate, thus they must use a form of outward expression. However, once we enter into the inner world of Unity, speech is no longer outwardly expressed. When one senses the Creator as a reality outside, there becomes a need for external expression: speech, body movement, and so forth. When a person awakens to Unity, speech becomes more inward, until a total silence of body and voice is reached.

While this teaching addresses the spiritually-evolved student, who senses Unity within, The Baal Shem Tov also teaches the novice about rapid bodily movement and screaming as valid pathways of devotion. Through these expressions *Hislahavus*, "conflagration", ecstasy, or rapture is generated.

[Excerpted and Translated from the 'Ohr Ha'Emes']

The Baal Shem Tov said: "When a person is drowning in water and he moves wildly about to free himself from drowning, certainly onlookers will not laugh at his bodily gestures. Similarly, when a person is praying and makes wild body movement and contortions, we should not mock him, as he is trying to save himself from the sinful waters that are drowning him, which are the negative, intruding thoughts that are entering his mind to distract him from prayer".

(Ohr Ha'Emes, Imrei Tzadikim, p. 83b).

Upon entering onto the path of prayer, one shows more bodily movement and external rapture. This eventually leads to a place of unity and stillness.

[Excerpted and Translated from the 'Tziva'as Harivash']

"Prayer is like being intimate with the Shechinah, the "Divine Presence" within creation. Just as within the first steps of intimacy there is more movement, and gradually the movement subsides, the same is with prayer. At first one needs to move about bodily, and then later he can stay still, in one place, with no outer movement, as he enters into a state of Deveikus with the Shechinah, and All is One."

(Tziva'as Harivash, 68).

As we see from the next two selections, on the one hand he is speaking of praying very quickly, reciting each word with rapid succession, as a person on fire for Hashem.

[Excerpted and Translated from the 'Amud HaTefilah']

"Sometimes a person can say the words of prayer so quickly, and the reason is because his heart is on fire, burning with a love to Hashem, and the words tumble out his mouth, as if involuntary."

(Amud HaTefilah, 71).

While on the other hand, he also commends the one who prays without haste.

[Excerpted and Translated from the 'Tziva'as Harivash']

"Deveikus is when a person says each word of the prayers very slowly, drawing out each word. And that is because of his profound Deveikus with the actual words of prayer, he does not wish to part from them, so he clings to them, holding on to them and drawing them out."

(Tziva'as Harivash, 70).

IMMANENCE & TRANSCENDENCE

It appears that there are two ways of praying. One is with a loud voice in a rapturous display of emotions and overt bodily movements, demonstrating that one still senses a strong dichotomy, separation, and a powerful desire to get close. The other is being so inwardly-directed as to sense closeness with the Creator. The emotions become less revealed, the body gains more stillness and the voice quiets down until one reaches total Deveikus, unity, silence and oneness.

While these two states seem to contradict one another, they are in fact complementary. As the human brain is hardwired as a binary apparatus — an up-down, right-left, past-future paradigm — the brain automatically relegates the anything of the spirit to a purely transcendent, heavenly realm. When pondering the reality of a Creator, the brain attempts to measure that which cannot be measured. When it is realizes that the Creator is infinite while Creation is finite, the mind may seek to define the Creator as altogether separate and beyond any relationship to the earthly realm, thus defining the Creator as Transcendent.

But just as the Creator is unequivocally transcendent and beyond our grasp, the Creator is also manifest within the immanent earthly realm. The Creator simultaneously transcends and integrates all dualistic definitions: finite and infinite, form and formlessness, immanence and transcendence. The unity of G-d's essence is certainly beyond immanence, but also beyond infinity, beyond transcendence, and paradoxically, all-inclusive.

This is not an either-or question — Transcendent or Immanent, very far or very close, separate or unified. We need to relate to Hashem in both a state of Transcendence and a state of Immanence. We are the finite reaching out for the Infinite One, at once grasping for air, shaking and convulsing the body, raising our voice, shouting out and screaming out for the smallest taste of closeness; and also at the same time we are equally cognizant of the Creator within creation, giving birth to a calm silence and stillness, with no need for movement.

We are the pendulum swinging back and forth between closeness and distance, towards unity and then to separation. This is our life, a life with a body, physical matter, and a soul, spiritual reality. We are all contained within the tension of living a life being pushed and pulled in apparently opposite directions at once.

Regarding this existential paradox of being human, The Baal Shem Tov taught of a kind of dance, mirroring the dance of life, where the dancers move in and out. A circle is formed, a circumference with an empty middle. The movement of the dance is thus: First everyone who is in the circle goes to the furthest end of the circle, then all move towards the middle until they are face-to-face with each other, they then all move towards the outer part of the circle; this continues throughout the entire dance, they go back and forth, separating and reuniting *(Keser Shem Tov, Hosofos, 40, p. 15)*. This dance reflects life itself, mirroring the tension of separation and unity, immanence and transcendence.

Being a true master, a realized Neshamah Kelalis, the Baal Shem Tov embraced the path of wholeness — immanence and transcendence, body and soul, spirituality and physicality — not the path of either/or. Unity within Creation is an expression of the Unity of the Creator.

IN ALL YOUR WAYS

There is a short passage in scripture, which the sages of the Talmud say that all of the essential principles of Torah depend on *(Berachos, 63a)*.

"בכל דרכך דעהו". *Be'chal D'rachecah Da'ei'hu*, "In all your ways know Him" *(Mishlei, 3; 6)*. Simply, this instructs us to know and live with the Divine reality in all that we do.

Note that the three words begin with the Hebrew letters *Beis*, *Dalet* and *Dalet*, spelling the word *Badad*, the root of the word *Hisbodedus*. This is the classic Torah term for meditation *(Chidah, Avodos Ha'Kodesh)*.

This passage is intricately connected with a meditation practice. In all your ways, 'דעהו' *Da'eihu*, "Know Him". "Know", 'דע' *Da*, is used as a euphemism for intimate relations. Da'eihu thus means "knowing Him", cleaving to, being one with Him. Him is Hashem.

Along came along the Baal Shem Tov and said:

> *[Excerpted and Translated from the 'Tziva'as Harivash']*

> *"In all your ways know Him,' this is a great principle.* 'דעהו'*–"Know Him", is from the language that means connection, to connect the* ה*–Hei with the* ו*– Vav, in all your actions, even within physical things that you do."*

> *(Tziva'as Harivash, 94).*

The Baal Shem Tov is saying that we need to connect to Hashem, the immanence of the Creator within creation, at every moment and through every physical activity we do. We cannot reserve this connection only for prayer, study, meditation, or any of the other refined spiritual work. Everything needs to be included in this intimate connection.

A person who desires to connect with the Source, to lead a higher and deeper life, should not simply eat, sleep, work, and perform the mundane functions of life merely for gaining the strength or financial ability to later on dedicate his or her time to matters of the spirit.

We should not just pray, study, or meditate in order to spiritually connect. Rather, we should "know Him in all your ways." Eating, sleeping, working, using the restroom are all opportunities for Divine connection. The Baal Shem Tov teaches that using the restroom is a phenomenon of sifting out, removing the toxic and unusable from the good and purposeful. In fact all human activities can and should be an end unto themselves, not simply a means to an end, as they can all be an opportunity to "Know Him." Even the basic human drives can all be transformed into actions of *Yichud*, "unification", with Hashem.

The word *Hu* is spelled: הו, which means Him. These two letters are also the two final letters of the Name of Hashem, the Yud-Hei-Vav-Hei (י-ה-ו-ה). There are masculine and feminine letters. The Yud (dot) and the Vav (line) are masculine letters. The Hei-ה, which is formed as a kind of a receptacle, is the feminine. The masculine — not to be confused with the male — is the Transcendent, whereas the feminine is connected with the aspect of the Divine that is vested and manifest within creation, the Divine indwelling presence.

Da, we need "to know", to be intimate with and make a connection between the Vav, the masculine (giving principle, redemption, the world in its perfected reality), and the lower Hei, which is the presence of the Shechinah, of the divine indwelling which is the state of reality as is now.

The presence of the Shechinah can rise and fall, be exiled and redeemed. It is in a constant state of flux, depending on our reality and on the state of the world.

Everything that has been discussed above is actual meditative intention practices. These are ways of learning how to pray, eat, sleep and work with the proper Kavanah. And now that we have covered some basic elements of the Baal Shem Tov's approach, we will move to a more classical form of breath meditation.

SOUND- VIBRATION MEDITATION

Before we move into the world of breath, which is essentially the movement and circulation of air within our physical being, it is worth exploring the Baal Shem Tov's relationship to sound in general, and to the idea of the vibrations of sounds moving through the body in particular. This is true especially in prayer and also in Nigun.

There is a major *Chidush*, "novel approach", that the Baal Shem Tov revealed with regards to all meaningful speech and prayer especially, which is an elevated form of speech.

Great minds for millennia have pondered the deeper meanings of the traditional text of the Siddur, "liturgy". Knowing that the liturgy was formed and founded in great holiness and with Ruach Ha'kodesh, "holy spirit", each word and letter was analyzed, deciphered and decoded. The words we speak in prayer are the channels upon which the energy of creation, history and redemption flow. We are completing a circuitry, from Above to below, and from below back to Above. In order to pray/play properly in such a cosmic symphony of creation, one must learn to read the notes and practice the scales. The bulk of previous kabbalistic writings on prayer throughout the ages focused on the shapes of the letters, their numerical value, or the amount of letters and words within a phrase or passage, attempting to uncover the hidden roots of each word.

The Baal Shem Tov opened up a different, original path. Instead of the left-brain approach, which is linear, cerebral and intellectual, the path that the Baal Shem taught was more right-brain oriented, relating to the very sounds and vibrations of the words and letters themselves. Even deeper, the approach is meant to sense the truth of what one is saying, not just in the mind, but to feel the truth of one's words in their body.

One of the novelties of the Baal Shem Tov's teachings is that the fundamental principle of Hashem's unity is not merely an idea to contemplate, but a spiritual understanding of the mind to be felt in the heart and experienced in the body. The truth of the Unity of the Creator is to be sensed on all levels of existence.

INHALE/INTENTION
EXHALE/ EXPRESSION

The two words *Baruch Ata* mean: "You are the Source of all Blessing". One begins a blessing by taking a deep inhale, and while inhaling, ponder the meaning of these words during a short pause. Then in the exhalation, bring all focus to the words Baruch Ata. The exhalations are extended for the vibrations of the words to penetrate the body and for each letter to be visualized as it is articulated in the outbreath. Through this practice, breathing becomes a conscious feedback, circulating Divine energy from the Source back into to you; from the Higher into the Lower on the inhale, and from you to the Source, the lower to the higher, returning in the exhale.

Prayer and all manner of speech are transformed from a conceptual, even dualistic, exercise of the mind into a non-dual, all-encompassing fullness of existence — prayer reverberating integrally on all levels of mind, heart and body.

ENTER FULLY INTO EACH WORD

There is profound beauty and depth in simply being with the letters themselves. At the time of the Great Flood, Noach, or Noah, was told, *Bo El Ha'Teiva*, "You shall enter the Ark". *Teiva*, says the Baal Shem Tov, means "ark", but also means word. Hashem is telling Noach, and us, to enter fully into the words we speak. Not only should we know what we are saying and speak with wisdom and mindfulness, but we need to enter into that speech with our entire being — thoughts, feelings, sensations, and energy — into the words we that we say/pray. We need to feel all the light, energy and sweetness of every movement of sound.

The sacredness of the holy sounds and vibrations from the letters of the words we say needs to infuse us completely. We should feel the sounds and movements entering and exiting our bodies.

The actual practice is as follows: Inhale, think of the meaning of the word Baruch. Pause, then slowly exhale: Baruch-hhhh. Or even, exhale baaaaa. Pause, inhale. Then exhale ruuuuchhhh. Inhale, think Ata, exhale Ataaaaa, or, Aaaaaaa. Pause, inhale. Then exhale, Taaaaaa.

With every word we say and even with every letter, we experience the sounds vibrating throughout our bodies and consciousness.

If one finds that it is too challenging or time-consuming to pause at each letter or word, one can pause before reciting every two or three words. In fact, countless sources suggest that one should never utter more than two to three words at a time during prayer. Either way, it is recommended to take a moment to pause, reflect on the meaning of the following few words, secure a proper Kavanah, and then recite them. The pause enables us time for reflection. The uniqueness of the Baal Shem Tov's path is that when one actually recites a few words after the inhale and pause, one needs to let go of the mental activity of intention and merely be with the sounds and words when they are expressed on the exhalation.

It is even appropriate and beneficial at times to say the entire blessing on one powerful extended exhalation, especially if one is struggling with extraneous thoughts disrupting focus (Ohr HaGanuz, Bechukosai). Before saying a blessing, deeply inhale and think of the meaning of the words of the blessing, and then recite the entire blessing in one out-breath.

This is a very simple, yet transformational way of saying blessings or utilizing prayer. There is no thinking while the words are being spoken. This frees up all one's strength of concentration to animate the letters, words and sounds.

This path of prayer transfers the vibrational energy of the Aleph Beis from the prayers in the book to our bodies in a tangible way to the point where we are fully absorbed within a reverberating field of holy sound; we are within our holy *Teiva*, "Word/Ark".

We must enter fully into the letters in order to feel their sensations coursing through the body, activating the life within each sound as we pray with these words. In prayer, we open ourselves up to be thoroughly immersed within each letter and to receive the life renewing properties that are found within the Aleph Beis.

EACH LETTER CONTAINS WORLDS

The letters of the Aleph Beis, the Hebrew Alphabet, contain their own power as they are the building blocks of creation. The letters are the fundamental underlying movements, murmurs, vibrations, and energies of creation. When we say the words and letters of the prayers we are tapping into the cosmic energy of creation. Paradoxically, by simply praying with the letters and words alone, just chanting them without intellectual intention, one harnesses the deepest Kavanah of what the words mean and represent.

The Baal Shem Tov teaches that if one were to meditate and entertain a particular Kavanah in depth while reciting a word of prayer, whatever is captured by one's capacity of thought is how much he has. Contrary to this, someone who is praying with the letters/words themselves, this person has everything because the deepest meanings lay within the vibration of the letters/words themselves.

THE MASTER KEY

If the earlier Kabbalists and sages gave us all the individual keys and combinations to all the doors of the inner workings of creation in the form of the idea of the Yichudim, the sacred name combinations, the Baal Shem Tov gave the world the one master key that unlocks all doors *(Likutim Yekarim, Likutim Chadashim, 197)*. The master key is the letters/ words themselves. The potency of the sounds of the letters and words is the most powerful element in creation.

In a similar vein, once before Rosh Hashanah the Baal Shem Tov summoned his student Reb Ze'ev and instructed him to study the deep Kabbalistic intentions so that he can blow the Shofar for everyone in synagogue. With excitement and focus Reb Ze'ev dedicated every waking hour to delving into the teachings and mystical Divine names connected with the Shofar. In order to remember everything he was learning, he wrote notes for himself and kept them in his prayer book. On the morning of Rosh Hashanah, as Reb Ze'ev was walking to the synagogue, his prayer book opened. Unbeknownst to him, his notes slipped out. When the time came to blow the Shofar, Reb Ze'ev opened the prayer book and to his disbelief the notes were nowhere to be found. Dumbfounded and overcome with grief, he began weeping. With a truly broken heart, he picked up the Shofar, made the blessings and managed through his tears to blow the required sounds. After the prayers, the Baal Shem Tov came over to him and complimented him for the most wonderful and deepest Shofar blowing he had ever heard.

And then the Baal Shem Tov explained: In the place of the king there are many chambers and each door has its own distinct key. The deeper Kabbalistic intentions are the keys to the rooms. There is, however, a master key that opens all doors, and that is a broken heart.

The power of the sound of the Shofar is the simple broken sound itself. Similarly, the letters and words contain all of the deepest, most profound intentions. To truly access all their power and profundity, one simply needs to recite each letter and word with all the strength of their being, completely entering into each sound.

ASIYAH, YETZIRAH, BERIAH, ATZILUS
WORDS, SONG, SUBTLE AWARENESS, SILENCE

Without unleashing the veritable flood of details that each of these four worlds/perspectives represent, here is the most basic synopsis: The lowest is the physical reality, above this is the emotional world, even higher is the mental world and above this is the spiritual world. In the course of praying with the letters/words themselves, we move through these four worlds.

We lose ourselves completely within the sounds of the letters and the letters are strung together becoming words, and the words together become like a great symphony of multiple harmonies and sounds, reverberating and resonating through our consciousness.

What began as the sound of a single letter, becomes a word, and then many words and many sounds. This is the movement from a single letter or word, the physical world, into many words; from a single sound into multiple sounds, like music, this is the emotional world. Our emotions are aroused by the sounds of the stringing together of the various letters and words, as they become a song, made up of musical notes. There is an inner joy and pleasure one receives when gently moving from one sound into the next, like the art of playing cords of music.

Slowly these sounds of music become background noise and one enters deeper into a more inward reality, a more subtle, still, introspective space. One very pronounced sound becomes many sounds strung together, almost like a rhythm of music, slowly, the sounds become more streamlined until it becomes like a hum, similar to the sound of waves someone would hear near the ocean. And then, in organic fashion, the hum becomes quieter and quieter. There is eventually a collapse of all noise, both external and internal, a total quieting of the mind, of thought, feelings and sensations as one attains a measure of total inner stillness, a measure of Deveikus, unity with the Source of all Unity.

MUSIC- SONOROUS AIR

Thinking about air, breath, sounds, and vibration it behooves us to at least mention the idea of music, since the practice of singing and playing music is intricately connected with the Baal Shem Tov and the movement he inspired. Music is a form of sonorous air, harmonious vibrations.

Music is a big conversation which was explored in great detail in a previous book called: *Inner Rhythms: The Kabbalah of Music*, and will be further explored as a meditative practice in a future book. For now, let us touch upon it shortly in order to understand its power from a meditative paradigm, as well as in relationship to the profound teachings of the Baal Shem Tov.

Music uplifts, inspires, and deeply transforms the listener, and is a medium for inner transportation, taking one on an inner journey to worlds and places deep and beyond.

"There are chambers in Heaven which can only be opened through song" *(Tikkunie Zohar, Tikkun 12)*. Music unveils realities that are otherwise not so easily reachable.

Since time immemorial, the playing of instruments has been an integral ingredient to assist in heightening consciousness. The Biblical prophets of old would use music to induce a meditative and prophetic state. In the words of a master prophet, "Now play for me the instruments of music ...and when the musician will play....the hand of Hashem will be affixed" *(Melachim 2, 3:15)*. The playing of music initiated the prophetic state, expanding the consciousness of the prophet in order to receive prophetic influx *(Rambam, Hilchos Yesodei HaTorah, 7:4. Akeidas Yitzchak, Shemos, Shar 35)*.

There is a dual purpose for the playing of music. Beyond the power of music to clear distracting thoughts, music also uplifts the meditator *(R. Avraham Ben Ha'Rambam. HaMaspik L'Ovdei Hashem, Hisbodedus)*. After musically inducing an altered state of consciousness, the potential prophet is readied for the Divine flow to rest upon them.

There are even sources that are of the opinion that music was not only used to induce a prophetic or expansive state of mind, but rather that the playing of the music was done throughout the entire prophetic experience. Music continued to be played as the prophet prophesized. Because, music is the movement of air in a very refined genteel manner, this is the language of the inner/upper realms *(Avodas HaKodesh, Cheilik Ha'Tachlis, 10. Menos Levi (Alkebatz) Hakdamah. Divrei Yisrael (Modzitz) Miketz).* Music is the speech of angels, it feels Divine While listening to or playing deep music we get a sense of transcendence, of tapping into something that is beyond us, and all the while we are fully present in our immediate reality.

The power and magic of music is not found in its ecstatic anti-rationality, but rather in its link to transcendence. Perhaps it is not the transcendence within the music itself, but rather the reaction to the music, the transcendence reached as one reacts to music.

Music and the *Nigun*, the "wordless tune", are synonymous with the Baal Shem Tov and his teachings.

Beyond the potential prophetic, expansive, or simply ecstatic state that music and song can stimulate, which the Baal Shem and his students certainly used, the hallmark of the teachings of the Baal Shem Tov are Light, Joy and Love.

Light — that the whole world is filled with Divine Light;

everything, every person, and every situation is filled with Hashem's light, albeit sometimes hidden. Joy — knowing this deeply and trusting that Hashem is with us always, whenever and wherever we are brings one to joy. All the while Love should be the foundation of one's life; a love of the Creator and thus by extension a love for all of creation, as Hashem's love permeates all of existence.

Joyful music brings more joy, and one who is joyful enjoys music. The same is true with love, one who is in love sings love songs; even one who is out of love sings the blues *(Sefer Chareidim, 10:6)*.

In this way, one needs to choose the type of music he surrounds himself with or sings. If the objective is expansive states of mind, a meditative and contemplative Nigun should be chosen. If one needs to feel more joy in life, an upbeat rhythm may do the trick. If one wishes to enter into a more silent form of meditation and contemplation a wordless Nigun that moves from a louder to a quieter place is in order.

Music and Nigun can be used to induce and stimulate a particular state of consciousness, and it can also be employed to accompany the actual meditation. It can even be used on its own, as a sound-based vibrational method of meditation and practice.

TWO FORMS OF
BREATHING TECHNIQUES
....

Let us return to simple breath.

There are two forms of breathing techniques. There is the complex path of the 13th century Spanish Kabbalist, Rabbi Avraham Abulafia, where the meditator chants various letters with specific respiratory patterns, as well as head maneuvers corresponding to the directions of the particular vowel that is being chanted. This practice is very elaborate. For example, if one is breathing out the sound of Uuh - a vowel that is placed in front of the Hebrew letter, they would move their head forward. If they were chanting the Eee sound - a vowel that is placed on the bottom of the letter, they would move their heads downwards.

This detailed practice demands over an hour of time, and sometimes up to seven or eight hours, to complete in one sitting. R. Abulafia's method of breath meditation will be discussed at great length in a future text in this series.

The second method, the one we are concerned with now, is much simpler. That being said, it is not less profound, just more accessible. The main aspect of this practice is to become aware of one's breath unrelated to any other sounds or sights.

Breathing is the most essential process of life, and yet, most often the least noticed. Breath is life. It is free and always with us. It is the one constant of life — wherever we are, whatever we are doing, we are always breathing. All of life rises and falls within the context of our breath.

An awareness of breath brings us to a state of Yichud. A mere reflection on how we breathe helps us realize the porous boundary between the self and others, and truly the whole world around us. Breath flows in and out of us, circulating continually within and through us into all of life that surrounds us. Breath is the experiential manifestation of the total symbiotic and reciprocal relationship that exists between us and the whole world around us.

We cannot live without air and respiration, and for that we need the healthy air that we are in. Furthermore, we would not be alive for more than an instant if not for the constant atmospheric pressure that holds our bodies together. If not for the pressure from the air that surrounds us we would literally blow apart. There is a give and take in both directions with the air and the environment we are in.

One of the wonders of simply becoming aware of the breath is the recognition of our total dependency. Through conscious breathing we have a clear awareness of the interconnectedness of all life, how we are dependent on our environment and need healthy surroundings to survive and thrive. This awareness helps us to unlearn the erroneous view that we each exist independently. Breathing, in the most overt way, shows us that we need the outside oxygen for our inside breath to exist.

We need, and more deeply are actually one with, the atmosphere that encircles us. Contemplating this truth helps us understand that we need and are one with the Source of that atmosphere, the Creator of all of life. We need and are one with the divine animating and encircling light that continually creates and sustains creation.

THE BAAL SHEM TOV ON BREATH

Let us get into this a little deeper. We will begin with a quote from the Baal Shem Tov, as recorded by his students:

[Excerpted and Translated from 'Amud HaTefilah']

Let us first understand that the word in Hebrew for "breath", Neshimah, is closely related to the word Neshamah, "soul". In this way the breath is the appropriate vessel through which a person can uncover the root of his soul.

"Certainly, when a person's prayers are refined, then the holy breath that emanates from his mouth will merge and connect with the Supernal Breath which enters his body at all times. Concerning the verse

from Psalms which states that: "The Neshamah of every living being shall praise Hashem (Tehilim, 150)," our sages say: "With Every Neshima and Neshima, "breath and breath", a person takes he shall praise Hashem. This breath he takes travels from the bottom Upwards and then returns from Above to below. And certainly he is able to easily connect the part of Divinity that is within him to its Source."

(Amud HaTefilah. 27, p. 111).

What does this mean? What is the Supernal Breath? What does it mean that the breath we breathe enters us from Above, and that we then return our breath to the Above?

Let us begin with the narrative of the creation as related in the Torah.

FROM UNITY TO DUALITY:
THE COSMIC MOVEMENT FROM STILLNESS TO SOUND

To begin we need to start by unearthing the process of creation. What had to occur for there to be a movement from absolute Unity to a world of seeming duality and dichotomy — up-down, right-left, before-after, past-future, black-white?

The Torah describes creation as a process of Ten Divine Utterances. It is through these primary utterances that creation emerges and is manifest. "G-d said let there be light, and there was light." The world of duality begins with speech, when thought becomes word.

The grand metaphor for the emergence of creation is via divine speech. Speech is a movement from the inside-out. Think about human speech. When we speak and communicate our feelings to another we are taking something from inside us and through speech, revealing it to the outside, to another.

Speech moves feelings, ideas, and whatever else is going on within the interior to the exterior. Speech takes the internal and makes it external.

The One is now being expressed within the many. Duality, an inside and an outside, is thereby created.

Beis, which is the second letter of the Hebrew Alphabet, is the first letter in the Torah. The Torah begins with the letter Beis. Because creation by definition is a two, an externalization of that which was formerly inside, the Torah begins with the second letter. The word creation itself implies a duality, as in a Creator above who creates the creation. This dualistic creation operates within a dualistic, separated consciousness, giving birth to the perception of a past and future, an up and down, right and left, good and evil, me and you, us and them, and so forth ad infinitum.

The creation of duality is through speech — a divine vibration of metaphysical sound — which gives rise to a physical vibration of energy, which is then transformed and solidified as matter.

Beneath, beyond and within the dual reality of speech there is a world of Unity, the world of Thought, the world of the Aleph, the world of Atzilus. This world of thought is the way all exists within the mind of the Creator, metaphorically speaking, before being externally articulated and manifested through speech.

Before the world of Speech is the world of Thought, and before Thought is only ONE.

Within the *Ein Sof*, the "Infinite Light of One", a thought arises to create an other outside of Oneself. In this world of thought, Atzilus, there is an entire conceptive structure of what this other will look like and how it will function. Much like before you create something you have an idea in your mind about what you would like to create, and then you actually go ahead and create it.

First there is the inner movement within the Mind of the Creator, giving rise to a desire and will to create within the stillness of the Ein Sof. This conception of existence is still within the reality of Unity, as it is a movement within the mind, as it were, of the Creator.

This is the world of *Atzilus*, of "nearness". There is a something, a conception of an other, yet it is totally consumed and absorbed within the Creator's mind.

SPEECH -WIND -BREATH:
THREE STAGES OF A DUALISTIC CREATION:

Thought becomes speech, and creation within the mind of the Creator becomes a separate physical reality. These are the two basic paradigms: The world of thought/interior and the world of speech/exterior. In greater detail, there are three stages necessary for thought to become word, for the inner to become outer, and for unity to become apparent duality.

A closer reading of the Genesis narrative reveals that while most of creation is created through speech and utterances, there is another method for creation; and that is when the Torah narrates the creation of Neshamah, "souls". When the Creator created the human being it says, "He blew into his nostrils a breath of life, and man became a living being" *(Bereishis 2:7)*. Souls are created through breath.

There is a third image, a third means of creation, as it says in the book of Psalms, "By the word (speech) of Hashem the heavens was created and all the Angels therein by the Wind of his mouth" *(33:6)*.

There are three forms and movements from thought into word: breath-wind-speech.

- The "Physical World," *Olam*, is created through Speech
- The world of *Malachim*, "Angels," is created through Wind
- The world of *Neshama*, "Souls," is created through Breath

These are not merely three defined but unconnected realities. Rather, they represent three layered stages of consciousness and measures of separation. These are three perspectives, each one deeper than the next.

World is created through speech. This is the reality of strong duality. The perspective and sensation of a person functioning from this state of reality is that of separation. From the place of world, the created being, the human, reaches out to connect with G-d, the Creator, who is above and beyond. Here is the place of independence, of total free choice.

Angels are created through wind. Functioning within the reality of angels there is a sensation of being like the wind within the mouth of the Creator. There is some sense of separation, like a wind swirling within the mouth of G-d, yet, one gets the sensation of being completely absorbed by the Creator's light. Here there is still some measure of free-choice, not whether to act or not, but how to act.

Souls are created through breath. Operating within the reality of souls is to sense oneself as if being within the divine gut as it were, the Divine diaphragm, so to speak. In the lungs, before the wind, the air rises into the mouth. This is a very subtle, created world and perspective. On the one hand it is a creation and yet it has an overwhelming apprehension and sensation of its Creator. Here there seems to be a blending between being a creation and being in total unity with the Creator. The spark of the Creator and the spark of creation are unified.

These three realities — of souls, angels and world — need to be understood not as distinct types of creations, but rather every form of existence contains these three to four layers or potential perspective as every word originates from wind, and every wind originates from breath.

Breath, wind, and certainly externalized speech, are the three layers, one within the other, of creation. Breath becomes speech *(Sefer Maamorim t'r't't, Rayatz, Karov Hashem)*. Before there is breath, there is the thought to breathe. Creation first begins within the Mind of the Creator as an idea. This is the world of Atzilus.

The thought then becomes externalized, first as breath within the lungs of the Creator, metaphorically speaking.

This is the world of *Beriah*, "creation".

Then the world becomes more external as a free flowing wind within the mouth of the Creator. This is the world of *Yetzirah*.

Then the world becomes seemingly externalized from the Creator as the world of speech, the world of *Asiyah*.

FOUR PERSPECTIVES & STATES OF CONSCIOUSNESS

Speech is when we sense separation. A Creation connected to, though separate from, the Creator. The sensation is that we, the creation, exist and are guided by the Creator.

Wind is when we sense being enveloped within the Creator.

Breath is when we sense being not only enveloped, but literally within, deep within the Creator.

Thought is where there is only One, we do not feel any separation.

PERSPECTIVE ONE: THE SPEECH/OLAM/WORLD PARADIGM

The nature of speech is that it reveals our thoughts and

feelings outwardly, but the link between the spoken word and the person who spoke the words is tenuous at best.

Say, for example, your spouse or child tells an idea to someone and, later on, that person comes to you and tells you over their idea without saying who originated the idea. If you are a perceptive person, and if you know your spouse or child well, you will say, "this sounds like something my spouse or child would say". But what happens if that same idea is told to a third person, a person that does not know your spouse or child, than they would think that the person giving over the idea is the originator of the idea, or he heard it from someone, but have no inkling who.

The same is true with creation on this level and paradigm of existence. The Creator speaks the world into existence. If we are intimate with G-d, if we have a relationship with the Creator, than we see the hand of the Creator within every aspect of creation. In other words: Within the speech we recognize The Speaker, the originator of the speech. It is as clear to us as when someone repeats something our spouse or child said, without saying who said it.

Yet, the less one cultivates a relationship with the Creator, the less he sees the Creator within creation. Atheism is a real possibility in a world created and sustained by Divine speech.

The perspective of Asiyah is that there is a creation, a very real apparent independent creation, and this creation is created by the Creator. There is a divide, a clear dichotomy, and the two are in relationship with each other.

PERSPECTIVE TWO:
WIND / MALACH/ ANGEL PARADIGM

Here one experiences an even deeper sense of closeness with the Creator. Not just that G-d is the Creator, but in this state one actually feels angelic, as if they were completely absorbed and enfolded within the Divine. Much like any deep relationship where one begins by feeling separate and gradually gets closer and closer until, at some point, they become, hopefully (although only for a period of time), so in love with the other that they lose themselves within the other; they feel absorbed within their lover's embrace.

In this paradigm one feels like an angel, which represents a reality where one is completely like the wind fluttering within the mouth of the Creator. One feels like they are swimming within the Divine reality.

PERSPECTIVE THREE:
BREATH/ NESHAMAH/ SOUL PARADIGM

Here one experiences an even deeper sense of closeness with Hashem. Beyond being enveloped, surrounded, or floating within, as wind within the mouth of Hashem, as it were, one feels literally submerged within the deepest reality of the Divine; they are nestled within the essence of the divine womb, in the stomach, the root of breath. There is a certain sensation that the I, the separate 'i', is diffusing and melting into the Divine I, the Ultimate I.

PERSPECTIVE FOUR: THOUGHT/UNITY PARADIGM

This is the deepest layer. Here there is no longer any I. There is no more separate self, no independent existence, no Yesh. There is no-thing to experience. There is no experiencer, no I to register the experience. One is one with the One and is so with no awareness of such unity. The experiencer is one with the experienced. Not that "I am connected to the Creator", or "enveloped" or even "lost within"; but rather, there is no I.

These are four experiential perspectives within our relationship with the Creator. Each one is deeper than the next.

CONTINUOUS CREATION

Creation is continuous. Every moment there is the cosmic exhale from the Creator that begins as a Thought and then evolves into Breath, to Wind, and then to Speech, which in turn creates energy, and energy solidifies into matter.

From the Thought to create comes the Breath of Life as in, "He blew into his nostrils a breath of life", *(Bereishis 2:7)*. This is followed by the Wind within the Mouth, which gives birth to Divine Speech, as in, "G-d said, let there be light, and there was light" *(Bereishis 1:3)*.

First there is an inner movement within the Unity of the Creator, as it were, which then moves and becomes un-differentiated breath, then wind, then Divine articulation — differentiated and particularized speech. The words of this speech are the spiritual, meta-physical vibrations that trigger corresponding physical vibrations, energy and eventually matter.

These four Stages of Creation correspond to the four letters in the essential Name of G-d in the Torah, the *Yud-Hei-Vav-Hei*, also referred to as Hashem, "The Name".

1) Inner Movement/Desire/Thought—Unity— Yud (י).
2) Breath—Souls — Hei (ה).
3) Wind—Angels—Vav (ו).
4) Speech —Physical world — Hei (ה).

FOUR LEVELS OF CREATION:

Inner movement
Breath
Wind
Speech

THIS CORRESPONDS TO THE FOUR INNER WORLDS:

Creation from speech, physicality, *Asiyah*, the world of Actualization.

Creation from wind within the mouth, angels, *Yetzirah*, the world of Formation.

Creation from breath, soul, *Beriah*, the world of Creation.

Movement within the mind, thought, *Atzilus*, the world of Nearness.

THESE FOUR INNER WORLDS ALIGN WITH THE FOUR LETTERS :

When a person has a will and desire to speak, to articulate and express, this is a movement of the speech within his heart/mind. This is Atzilus and the small letter Yud.

When the speech reaches the chest as breath it is the world of Beriah, the expansive letter of Hei

When the speech reaches and fills the mouth, it is the world of Yetzirah, the letter Vav.

When the speech and voice become manifest words, coming out of the month, it is the world of Asiyah, the final expressive and expansive letter of Hei.

Everything in our universe has a unique space, structure, sound and rhythm. Everything has a distinct kind of vibration. The multiple things we observe with our senses are physical manifestations of their respective Divine frequencies. In fact, in Hebrew there is no word for "thing". It is merely called De'var, "word" or utterance. Every-thing is essentially a product and physical manifestation of a unique Divine vibration/word.

OUR INHALE – COSMIC EXHALE/
OUR EXHALE – COSMIC INHALE

Since creation is continuous and creation begins with a thought, breath, wind, speech, thus, in every moment there is the cosmic exhale of the Creator into the world — from a thought to create, to a breath, to a wind, to speech, which creates energy and energy becomes matter.

When we inhale we enliven ourselves. On a deeper level, what we are doing when we inhale is inhaling the Cosmic, Supernal Exhale that is right this moment enlivening, animating, and sustaining creation.

Conversely, when we exhale, we are returning our life force to the Supernal Breath. Every exhale is a momentary death, a returning and emptying of ourselves into the Divine Inhale.

Our out-breath is emptied into the Cosmic inhale, and our in-breath is inhaling the Cosmic exhale. We breathe in new life force that is given to us, and we empty ourselves back into our Source. There is a constant in and out, a reciprocal reflection of each other. What is exhaled and given to us is the new Chayus Eloki, the "Divine life force" that is flowing into creation. We inhale and we then exhale, returning that which has enlivened us back to its, and our, Source.

EVERY MOMENT A NEW LIFE FORCE IS EXHALED INTO CREATION

Creation is continuous. Every year — and more deeply — every month, every day, every hour and truly every moment a brand new revelation of Divine light is being revealed into the world that creates, sustains and animates creation anew.

Every moment there is a renewed vitality, a Divine energy that is injected into the universe. Every year, month, day and moment resonates with a particular, distinct divine frequency. A very specific frequency vibrates at this very moment, distinctive from any other moment of creation.

Every year there is a new and deeper revelation of Hashem's presence and light in creation. The world is spiritually evolving, moving closer and closer to the experience and expression of divine unity.

SEVEN THOUSAND YEAR CYCLE

Human history is subdivided into a seven thousand year cycle.

Each unit of a thousand years corresponds to another day of the seven-day cycle of creation, which in turn corresponds to one of the Seven Emotive Sefiros, the Divine attributes.

A note about the Sefiros:
The ten sefiros are like screens through which the Infinite Light of the Creator penetrates and creates finite reality. The distinct forms, shapes and colors of the sefiros serve as filters through which the infinite colorless, formless, unified light is reflected into our world. Passing through the sefiros causes the light to appear differentiated and colored. The word *Sefira*, from the word meaning 'counting', is also related to the word meaning "edge", as in the edge of the city, as each Sefira is a measured, counted, and finite, edge. The sefiros are the screens that allow the Infinite Light to be 'measured' and finite in this world. The word Sefira is also from the word *Sipur*, meaning "story". They thus tell the story of creation, of the Infinite Light becoming manifest in finite

form. And finally, the word Sefira is also related to the word *Sappir*, "illuminated", like a Sapphire. Thus the Sefiros are illuminated by the Divine Light as it passes through them on its way to finite manifestation. Additionally, by contemplating the Sefiros, and the story they tell, we too can be illuminated by the refraction of the Infinite Light through the prism of the Sefiros.

The Seven Emotive Sefiros are:
- Chesed – kindness, love, giving
- Gevurah – strength, restriction, judgment
- Tiferes – beauty, compassion, balance
- Netzach – victory, ambition, perseverance
- Hod – devotion, humility, acceptance
- Yesod – foundation, relationship, connection
- Malchus – royalty, receptiveness, presence

The first thousand years corresponds to Chesed, kindness and giving. The second thousand-year unit is Gevurah, restriction and judgment, and the next is Tiferes, compassion and balance, and so forth.

Every thousand years a new Divine light is revealed. First there was a revealing of Chesed. The next thousand years saw a revelation of Gevurah. Every millennium, there is another overarching divine energy being drawn down into the world and the universe resonates with a particular vibration and tone.

THE UNITS AND SUBUNITS
WITHIN ONE THOUSAND

Within each thousand years there are ten units of a hundred. Each of these ten units of a hundred years correspond to one of the Ten Sefiros - one of the three intellectual, mind sefiros, and of one the seven emotive sefiros.

The Three Mind Sefiros
* *Chochmah* – wisdom, intuition
* *Binah* –reason, cognition
* *Da'as*- knowledge, awareness

The first hundred years of the *Chesed* millennium, for example, correspond to the Sefira of *Chochmah*, wisdom and intuition; and the second hundred years of the Chesed millennium correspond to the Sefira of *Binah*, reason and cognition. Each year of the first hundred years reveal and express another aspect and dimension of the Chochmah of Chesed, the wisdom that guides kindness.

Within every unit of a hundred years there are ten units of tens. This is a deeper and more microscopic level of ten Sefiros within the ten. For example, the first ten years of the hundred within the thousand is the Chochmah of Chochmah of Chesed. And even more specific, the first year of the ten, hundred, and thousand, there is a revealing of Chochmah of Chochmah of Chochmah of Chesed. Every year within the greater cycle is a more refined and fine-tuned spiritual divine vibration. This demonstrates the kabbalistic principle of holographic inter-inclusion, wherein each part contains the whole.

Essentially, every year is a brand new year wherein a new Divine, enlivening, creative animating force is revealed.

EVERY MONTH, DAY AND HOUR
RESONATES WITH A DISTINCT FREQUENCY

Beyond the overall energy that flows into the new year, each of the twelve months of the year shine with another *Tziruf*, "combination of the four letters of Hashem's name", the Yud-Hei-Vav-Hei. Within the greater cycle of the year each particular month vibrates with a distinct divine frequency.

There are Four Letters in the Name of Hashem, the Yud-Hei-Vav-Hei. As mentioned, all Twelve months of the year have a distinct Tziruf or "permutation" of this most sacred name. Even though there are four letters in the Name of Hashem and four letters can create and be permutated into Twenty-Four different dimensions, still, since two of the letters are the same (there are two letter Hei's), with three letters the number of possible permutations is Twelve. For example: Yud-Hei-Vav-Hei, or, Yud-Hei-Hei-Vav, or, Yud-Vav-Hei- Hei, and so forth.

There are four seasons of the year — the spring, summer, fall and winter — these correspond to the four letters of the name. The Yud corresponds to the spring, the Hei with the summer, the Vav with the fall, and the final Hei with the winter *(Ramak, Pardes Rimanim, 21:16).* As such, the first triad of months, the three spring months, all begin with the first letter of the Name of Hashem, the Yud. The letter sequence of the first month is Yud-Hei-Vav-Hei. In the second month the Vav is placed as the last letter, forming the name as Yud-Hei-Hei-Vav. The third month the Hei is placed at the end, so the name would read as, Yud-Vav-Hei-Hei.

The second triad of months, the summer months, all begin with the second letter of the Yud-Hei-Vav-Hei, that is, with the letter Hei. The first month is Hei-Vav-Hei-Yud. The next month Hei –Vav-Yud-Hei, and the third month is Hei-Hei-Vav-Yud.

The third triad of months, the autumn months, all begin with the third letter of the Yud-Hei-Vav-Hei, that is the letter Vav. The first month is Vav-Hei-Yud-Hei, the second month is Vav-Hei –Hei-Yud, and the third month is Vav-Yud-Hei-Hei.

The fourth triad of months, the winter months, all begin with the fourth letter of the Yud-Hei-Vav-Hei, that is the letter Hei. The first month is Hei-Yud-Hei-Vav, the second month is Hei-Yud-Vav-Hei, and the third month is Hei-Hei-Yud-Vav.

The four-letter combination associated with each month represents a spiritual frequency, demonstrating what type of particular Divine energy flow is presently flowing into the world.

In the first month of the first year, there is a revealing of the Chochmah of Chochmah of Chochmah of Chesed that is shining through the prism of the letter permutation of Yud-Hei-Vav-Hei.

Even more specifically, and much more subtly, every day within the month, and even more detailed, every hour within the day reveals and is being enlivened by a distinct combination and permutation of divine light. The metaphysical reason there are twelve hours of the day and twelve hours of night is because the four letters in the Name of Hashem, the Yud-Hei-Vav-Hei, can create and be permutated into twenty-four patterns. Each hour of the day a variant combination of divine energy is manifest *(Shalah. Torah Ohr. Nosa, p. 21)*.

1,080 PARTS TO ONE HOUR AND 1,080 BREATHS

On the most subtle and refined level each moment resonates with its own inner divine frequency, one that was never present until this very moment. Within each hour itself there are 1,080 parts, which are called *Chalakim*. These 1,080 parts within each hour correspond to the 1,080 different possible combinations and permutations that can be created with the four letters of the Name of Hashem by adding the ten vowels into the equation. Each one of these four letters has ten possible vowels, thus in total 40. When you join these to each one of the 27 letters, 22 regular and five end letters, it equals 1,080. 40x27=1080. *

Each and every moment is being sustained by its own permutation of Hashem's name and its own vowel. For example, the Yud of the combination can be with the vowel Kametz, as in Ya-h, or Segul as in Yeh. Every moment of every hour within every day shines with a new revelation of Divine light that is revealed through the distinct permutation.

On average, a healthy mature adult takes about twelve to

---

* 1080 is also 5 times the word Gevurah. Gevurah numerically is 216. 5x216 = 1080. Gevurah is restriction. The dimension of time itself is a restriction. There are five levels of Gevurah, as in Chesed of Gevurah, Gevurah of Gevurah, Tiferes of Gevurah, and so forth, thus 1080. Yet, the eternal moment of time is also a revealing of Hashem, Infinite Oneness, expressed in the now. Time is also Chesed, a giving. Chesed in numerical value is 72. Ya-h, the essence and Chesed of Hashem's four-letter name, is numerically 15. 15 times 72= 1080.

twenty breaths per minute. The Kabbalistic number of breaths per minute is rounded out at eighteen, as eighteen is also written out as *Yud-Ches*, which spells the Hebrew word *Chai*, "life". In one hour, which is sixty minutes, the total is 1080. 60x18 = 1080 *(Reishis Chochmah, Shar HaYirah, 10. Although, R. Abulafia rounds up the number at 1000 breaths per hour. Ohr HaSechel, Chap 6).* Parenthetically, the total amount of breaths in a full day cycle is 24x1080=25,920; very close to the grand total of 26,000, as the name of Hashem equals 26.

Every year, month, day, hour and moment is truly new. No two moments are alike. Nothing is ever the same. Everything and everyone is new at every moment. With every single breath we inhale we are actually drawing in a completely new divine life force that was never drawn down to this world before. Something so marvelous, magnificent and miraculous occurs at every moment, and through the act of simply breathing we are –consciously – participating in this beautiful mysterious unfolding. Every moment a radically new permutation, combination, formation and information of divine creative life force creates and enters the world. With every inhale we are drawing inwards the newly revealed frequency that is pulsating at this very moment.

This indeed is the deeper meaning of the *Pasuk*, "verse", that proclaims, "A person does not live by bread alone, but from [the breath] that issues from Hashem's mouth" *(Devarim, 8:3).* Every moment we are inhaling the Divine outbreath that creates, sustains and animates creation anew at this very moment.

GOOD/HOLY BREATH
VS. NEGATIVE/UNHOLY BREATH

A closer reading of the original teaching of the Baal Shem Tov reveals something very profound and important, not just in terms of a meditative or contemplative practice of focused breathing, but also in terms of a fundamental understanding about life in general.

In the beginning of the quote from the Baal Shem Tov, the teaching begins with the words, *"When a person's prayers are refined, then the holy breath that emanates from his mouth will merge and connect with the Supernal Breath which enters his body at all times."* The simple question is why is this true only when a person's prayers are refined? And why only the holy breath? It would appear that our exhale returns into the Divine inhale no matter what words we speak in our outbreath.

There is another teaching by the Baal Shem Tov that may shed light onto this quandary. To quote his fantastical and gorgeous poetic words,

> *"When a person speaks good words, speech being the energy of the person and energy flows from the Cre-*

ator, then his words ascend Above and arouse the Supernal Speech, thus drawing down more energy from Above. When, however, a person speaks negative speech, then, as he speaks, his energy leaves him (as energy moves speech), and does not ascend Above. As such, he cuts himself off from all energy. As they say in Yiddish, "he let himself out" or, "he spoke and spent his energy"

(Baal Shem Tov, Torah, Bereishis, 102. Vayishlach, 13. Likutei Yekarim, 4b).

In general, in the perspective and viewpoint of the Baal Shem Tov, the definition of "good" is that which flows, moves, expresses, is life affirming, and giving. By contrast, the definition of bad is not ontological, but rather "bad" means the absence or blockage of flow, of light and giving, it is a state of stagnation and inertia.

In the above quote, the Baal Shem Tov clearly states that when a person speaks good words, meaning words of meaning that have a positive influence and constructive life affirming quality, then he is replenished by the arousal of Supernal speech that renews and revitalizes his energy. Yet, when he speaks bad speech, meaning, hurtful words, profanity, negativity, representing an absence of light and life, he ends up just spending and exhausting all of his energy, getting nothing in return.

There is a rhythm to creation. A Divine flow begins in thought, moves to breath, to wind, and then to speech. Eventually, a spiritual vibration evolves into physical energy, which creates, sustains and enlivens creation. When we inhale oxygen we are inhaling the Divine exhale. When we exhale and express, speaking positive words, we are continuing and tapping into the flow. The energy flows into us and we complete the circuitry by giving it out to others, essentially retuning the energy only to be replenished and rejuvenated with more vital energy.

Negative speech is fundamentally something that is rooted it some form of selfishness, ego, or self-interest, and it retains the energy, holding onto it, not releasing it outward, thus cutting off the circuitry and causing a form of energetic death, decay, and *Tumah*, "spiritual impurity". Imagine this in the form of a refrigerator plugged into the wall. So long as it is plugged into the socket the energy flows back and forth. Once the plug is pulled, the appliance has a short life span, as it is no longer being rejuvenated and revitalized.

All three levels of existence are layered, one perspective within the other. These three — speech, wind and breath, or, world, angel and soul — are all components of Lower Unity. There is also the reality of Atzilus, where we and creation only exist as a 'thought' within the Creator. In this reality, creation is mere *Ayin*, "no-thing-ness". This is Higher Unity.

TWO INTENTIONS:
THE I EXISTS VS. THE I DOES NOT EXIST

There are two levels of inner awareness: Higher Unity and Lower Unity. Higher Unity is more expansive and deep. Lower Unity is more restrictive and constrictive.

They are essentially different ways of seeing what is Above and what is Below. Higher Unity sees what is Above as Yesh, "existence" (True Existence or Divine Being), and perceives what is Below as Ayin, "nothingness" - nothing of substance, fundamentally a non-existent reality. Lower Unity sees the world below as the real Yesh (concretely, empirically existing), and perceives the Divine Source Above as Ayin - an imperceptible source, and thus, from its perspective, a no-thing.

In Lower Unity, my I/Ego exists, either as a world, angel or soul. Although I know that my existence is utterly dependent on the "thought" of the Creator to create and sustain to me, now that I am created, I exist. In Higher Unity, there is no separate I. I am within, as it were, the Thought of the Creator.

MEDITATION I

LOWER UNITY

....

BREATH MEDITATION

....

LET US BEGIN WITH THE LOWER UNITY PARADIGM WHERE THE 'I' EXISTS, ALTHOUGH I DO SENSE DEEPLY THAT MY EXISTENCE IS UTTERLY DEPENDENT ON THE CREATOR'S LIFE FORCE ANIMATING ME AT THIS VERY MOMENT.

AS A MEDITATIVE FOCUS AND CONSCIOUS awareness we can begin by imagining ourselves as a balloon that is being filled. Years back, some Kabbalists visualized the process of creation in terms of a Master Glass Blower blowing through his tube and filling the vessel *(Eitz Chayim, Shar Ta'n't'a, 5. Nefesh Chayim, Shar 1:15)*, for this reason we will use the balloon as a metaphor. Imagine being filled continuously by Divine cosmic outbreath, the moment the exhale ceases the balloon collapses, and in reality disappears as a balloon. When air is being pumped into the balloon, the balloon itself senses itself, as it were, as a serious, genuine existence. But we know better, we are aware that we are totally dependent on the breath of the blower that fills the tube with wind that creates Speech that gives rise to energy and thus to our matter, our very existence. We are like the balloon, so long as we are being filled we may get the impression of our total realness and independence, but, the moment the life force begins to dwindle, we awake to the awareness of our radical dependence on the Master Blower.

Let us gently close our eyes, or if you wish you can keep your eyes open, just stay focused and be mindful of your breath. As you inhale, meditate on how you are taking in the breath of life, rooted in the Source of all life. As you exhale, meditate on how this individual breath is returning to its Source in the Supernal Breath Above.

In the simple act of breathing we secure a clear awareness

of the total interconnectedness of all life with the Source of all life. We become acutely aware of how dependent we are on our environment and surroundings, how we need the world around us to live, and how we project ourselves and our energy through our exhale back into the living world around us.

This contemplation and meditation helps us to 'unlearn' and awaken from the dream that we exist as an independent entity. Breath in the most overt way shows that we 'need' the outside world for oxygen. Accordingly, we are thus able to see ourselves as one with the universe and the Ultimate Beingness that continues to give rise to the universe.

Essentially the idea is to live with this truth of unity, and see, hear, think and feel the Divine animating force within everything. We are completely dependent upon the Creator's life force, and each and every moment is a total *Chidush*, novelty.

The objective of the breath meditation is that not only should this powerful, transformative information of our dependency register intellectually in a mind space, but rather, we need to learn to make these truths our reality — to live and breathe it.

Here is a simple breath meditation that can assist us in this endeavor.

MEDITATION I:
LOWER UNITY - BREATHING
....
Letting go, Filling up
....
STEP BY STEP:
....

Every meditation begins with a commitment to honor the time you make for your practice. Clear space on your daily calendar, space in your home, space in yourself. Arrange the physical space to feel as inviting, warm and safe as can be.
....

Sit in your designated meditation spot comfortably and relaxed, but not overly relaxed that you may fall asleep. Closing your eyes is recommended.
....

Slightly lower your chin towards your chest to lengthen the back of your neck and switch gears to enter the parasympathetic nervous system, which promotes relaxation.
....

Take a moment for letting go of all the internal noise, chaos and movement. Simply be.
....

You may notice various sounds, bodily sensations, thoughts or feelings arise. Without manipulating or changing a thing, observe it all.

Guide your awareness to your breathing. Let the breath flow in and out through the nostrils.

Whether your breath is long, short, deep, shallow, slow or fast is not relevant. Let it be natural. If you feel uncomfortable by your breathing, adjust the rhythm accordingly.

The mind may wander. If so, gently return your awareness to the sensation of breathing. If you find yourself chasing after your thoughts, let them vanish as easily as they came and settle your attention on your breath.

As you inhale, meditate on gathering in the breath of life which is rooted in the Source of All Life, the Supernal Breath Above. Each inhale breathes into you new life, new vitality, new energy.

The inhalation is your experience of receiving the Divine Cosmic Exhale.

As you exhale, meditate on returning your individual breath to its Divine source, the Supernal breath.

....

The exhalation is your experience of giving yourself to the Divine Cosmic Inhale.

Embrace the awesome awareness that your entire existence is utterly dependent on the Creator's life flow of energy into this world.

Softly sit with this awareness for a few moments, as the breath smoothly flows in and out.

Seal your practice with gratitude for the chance to take part of this cosmic dance of breath.

Slowly reopen your eyes.

In the lower unity practice and consciousness the sense of separate self exists, but it is coupled with the awareness that our life is utterly dependent on the Life Force, the Cosmic and Supernal outbreath. There is a deep awareness that life does not exist without the continuous Divine exhale that animates our inhale.

MEDITATION II

HIGHER UNITY

. . . .

BREATH MEDITATION

. . . .

ONCE YOU HAVE SOMEWHAT MASTERED THE ABOVE TECHNIQUE YOU
CAN MOVE INTO MORE COMPLEX AND DEVELOPED PRACTICES.
THE PREVIOUS MEDITATION WAS A "LOWER UNITY" PRACTICE.
NOW LET US EXPLORE A "HIGHER UNITY" PRACTICE.

IN THE UPPER UNITY PRACTICE AND CONSCIOUS-
NESS there is no separate I, there is only YOU, there is only
One.

In this higher/deeper state of awareness there is no duality,
no separation, no dichotomy, no higher/lower, no above/
below, only unity.

In terms of breathing, there is no longer an I that is separate that is actively doing the breathing, rather just breath,
the supernal life force that enters and exists through me.

This state of consciousness is where one participates in the
prayer of all creation, hearing the Perek Shira, the songs
of Nature and the animals as every living thing with "every breath we take we sing the Creator's praise" (Medrash).
Not only does the revitalized new breath allow us to sing
the Creator's praise anew, but the breath itself, the pulsating movement flowing into and out of us is the Creator's
praise. Every new breath of life is another praise of the
Creator who creates, sustains and animates the living won-
drous creation.

BEING THE HEART OF THE WORLD

One slips into this state, moving from an I that is breathing
to breath that is simply breathing. Here one senses that he

is now the *Lev Ha'olam*, the "heart of the world", as it were. There is no longer a separate person who is breathing, rather, a sensation sets in, where you sense how your body never ends and you meld into the ground and space surrounding you. Everything around you feels like an extension. You become one with everything around you and your heart and breath are pumping a rhythm of life in and out of all reality.

One may begin this practice with a deep inhale and exhale. In the inhale draw down the breath from the nostrils to the chest, and then all the way to the bottom of the body, the tips of the toes. The exhale is reversed, pulling all the way from the tips of the toes, traveling through the torso, up the neck and out the nostrils. The drawing down and pulling up now begins to extend to outside the body. In the inhale, the drawing down extends beyond the toes into the floor, as it were; and in the exhale, one pulls energy from the entire room. Repeating this over and over, slowly, there is a certain sensation where one feels as if the entire room, the floor, the walls and everything in it is pulsating with their inhale and exhale. Everything is breathing with you, inwards, expanding in the inhale, and outwards, contracting in the exhale. Back and forth, in and out.

The world becomes animated and alive. Everything becomes rich, multi-textured and filled with vibration. You sense how everything is alive, pulsating, vibrating back and forth, and doing so in total synchronicity with the movement of your own heartbeat. Everything is breathing with you and through you. You are the center, the heart of the vibration of everything that is around. You are one with them and they are one with you. There is no separation between the interior and exterior, you are one with all of creation and ultimately with the Source of all life, the Divine animating energy that is flowing within and through you.

Here there is a dissolving of self. There is no longer a self that is aware of self and breath is simply moving in and out of you.

Meditation is a practice, and a practice suggests a doer, there is thus a separation between the doer and the doing. When there is a dissolving of the individuated self we actually cease meditating, or being aware of our breath; we simply allow and are the conduit through which the life force of creation flows within and through us.

Essentially, the Creator's Life Force is breathing through us, and we, as independent I's, do not exist. This is genuine Deviekus — losing the self-centered sense of separateness and becoming one with all of creation and the Creator.

On this level, there is no "you" who senses or feels the interconnectedness or unity, rather unity is simply what is. There is no I that is feeling connected to the divine life force flowing through you, rather it is just what is happening in the moment, spontaneously, effortlessly and simply. One becomes one with everything and the Divine breath merely flows within and through One.

MEDITATION II:

HIGHER UNITY - BREATHING

The Breath of Life Flowing Through You

STEP BY STEP:

Every meditation begins with a commitment to honor the time you make for your practice. Clear space on your daily calendar, space in your home, space in yourself. Arrange the physical space to feel as inviting, warm and safe as can be.

Sit in your designated meditation spot comfortably and relaxed, but not overly relaxed that you may fall asleep. Closing your eyes is recommended.

Slightly lower your chin towards your chest to lengthen the back of your neck and switch gears to enter the parasympathetic nervous system, which promotes relaxation.

Take a moment to center yourself in this moment, in this space, the here and now, the only moment there is. As you strengthen your center, the external chaos will dull and, with practice, fade away.

You may notice various sounds, sensations,

thoughts or feelings arise. Observe it all without manipulating or changing a thing.

Guide your awareness to your breathing. Let the breath flow in and out through the nostrils (unless you are congested, in which case, allow the breath come and go as need be without force).

If your mind wanders, gently return your awareness to the sensation of the breathing. If you find yourself following your thoughts, allow the thoughts to effortlessly drift away like clouds while you hold this steady space, your center. Keep focus on your breath as the mind settles.

As your sit in stillness, allow oxygen to flow in and out of you, open to the fluidity and aliveness that is within.

Here in this space, connect with the deep intimacy you share with the Creator of Life. The rhythm of your breath is the Divine flowing within you; it is as if you are sharing a dance.

Stop feeling, sensing or thinking, and allow the Supernal breath to flow through you.

Seal your practice from within this brilliantly subtle and ever-present Unity.

Slowly reopen your eyes.

THREE STAGES IN BREATHING:
INHALE/EXHALE/RETENTION

Up until this point the inhale and the exhale, and their relationship with meditative breath practices, have been explored, but breathing also includes a retention period between every inhale and exhale.

The retention is the in between stage, one is not inhaling or exhaling, just being.

There are three stages of breath: inhale, retention and exhale. The inhaling is called *Sheifah*, as in the word *Lishof*, to "aspire", as in aspiring to life and continued existence. The exhale is called *Neshifa*. And the retention is called *B'lima*, to "hold", or "nothingness". There is a retention, a pause, between every inhale and exhale, as well as between every exhale and inhale.

The *B'lima*, the retention stage is of crucial and of profound importance. There is tremendous potential in this in between state. It is within the moment of retention after the exhale, where one is empty of the past and not yet impregnated with the future — as one has not yet inhaled – where there is infinite possibility. The moment of retention is the kernel that contains all potential in terms of what Kavanah one will have when they inhale as well as what Kavanah one will hold when they exhale. In Hebrew the word for "retention", B'lima, also means "without what". In other words, there is no "what" yet in this stage; there is nothing determined or concrete, as it is still within the realm of possibility.

Retention is the most opportune time to fill the mind with positive, productive and holy thoughts. Select such a Kavanah and breathe in, internalizing this new found positivity. And then before the exhale, take one moment to meditate on what needs to be released, what is toxic that you are holding on to, such as a negative trait like anxiety, anger, or worry? Then expunge these toxins in the exhale.

Reb Shlomo of Zevil (1869-1945), the legendary Tzadik, speaks about the importance of the retention following an exhale. Once you empty your body in the outbreath, your body is now readied for a higher, deeper, holier, more productive inhale.

[Excerpted and Translated from the 'Menuchas HaNefesh']

"Each moment one draws in clear and pure wind/air (oxygen), and each moment one expunges (negative – carbon dioxide) wind from within him in the exhale, whether one is breathing short breaths or longer ones.

The (possible) exchange and renewal of thoughts is in the between stage, between the letting out the hot air (exhale) and the drawing in of new refined air (inhale).

If a person is careful and mindful at that moment
— in between the exhale and the new inhale — to
think only thoughts of holiness, than those thoughts
extend as long as the wind (the inhaled breath) lin-
gers within him.

One who becomes familiar with this practice and
does it often develops a good habit that becomes sec-
ond nature (meaning, the more one practices this
awareness while breathing, the more the awareness
will becomes his or her inner nature or default set-
ting). And one who comes to purify him or herself
receives helps from Above."

(Menuchas HaNefesh, p, 99).

Although there is only mention of the retention following
the exhale, retention or pause exists both prior and following every inhale and exhale. One may therefore expand the
three stages of breath into a four-part process, with the retention stage being repeated in between each successive inhale or exhale. This is similar to the way that the four-letter
name of Hashem (the Yud-Hei-Vav-Hei) is also actually
based on three individual letters, with the Hei being repeated before and after the Vav. If one were to overlay the
breathing process over the four-letter name, the retention
process would play the role of the Hei, coming in between
the Yud and the Vav, or the inhale and the exhale — inhale
(Yud), retention (Hei), exhale (Vav), retention (Hei) — re-

peat. In this way, we can say that we are actually "saying" the name of Hashem with each and every breath. Our very life itself is speaking this name, just as we are being spoken into being.

Yet, more broadly speaking there are three stages. Let us now move forward to get a better understanding of this three-prong process and its relationship with the Sefiros.

CHESED / OUTWARD COSMIC EXHALE
GEVURAH / INWARD COSMIC INHALE
A WORLD OF FREE CHOICE

There are these three stages: inhale, exhale, retention. What do they suggest, represent, and embody?

Earlier there was discussion of how the exhale reflects and mirrors the cosmic divine inhale, and the inhale mirrors the cosmic divine exhale. In effect, there are two movements: a cosmic outbreath, which creates, sustains, enlivens, nourishes and revitalizes existence, and a cosmic inhale, which pulls inwards, withdraws and essentially annihilates existence.

Every moment has both a dimension of the Divine attribute of Chesed — creating, giving, and expanding existence — and a dimension of the Divine attribute of Gevurah — restricting, retracting, rendering existence non-existent. Every moment of creation has both an element of creation and destruction, a filling with energy and a withdrawal, an eternal existential pendulum.

Chesed is the foundation of creation. The world is founded on Chesed, a Divine giving. The Divine desire of the Creator to create is an act of Chesed in and of itself — to give and create the possibility of an 'other.' Yet, if creation was a mere expression of Divine Infinite Chesed, without any Tzimtzum, "contraction" and concealment of Infinity, the world would never come into any apparent separate existence. Even if, somehow it would, it would be instantaneously overwhelmed by Infinity.

These two movements of Chesed and Gevurah — of giving, creating, and retracting, holding back — are the meta-source of our freedom to choose.

We all have the ability to create or destroy, to give love and light, or, heaven forbid, to spew hatred and darkness. We can give life and we can take life. Give to the world or take from the world. Contribute or receive. Protect the world and the planet or destroy the world and the planet. We can do so because there are two Divine forces, as it were, within the One. Of course both attributes are manifestations of the One at work in creating and maintaining creation. There is the force of Chesed, giving, and the force of Gevurah, restriction and holding back.

A MOMENT OF WRATH

The book of Tehilim, "Psalms", speaks about a Rega, a "moment", of (Divine) Apo, "anger" (30:6). In the Torah we find that Hashem tells Moshe, "If for one single Rega, "moment", I would go in your midst, I would destroy you" *(Shemos, 33:5)*. Rega is the moment of Din / judgment, of Gevurah, within each moment. The exhale dimension of every moment is an expression of Gevurah, restriction, withdrawal, which can appear as an element of Apo, "anger", destruction, undoing creation.

Additionally, our sages teach us that there is a moment of Divine anger once a day *(Berachos, 7a)*. What does this mean? Could it mean simply that within the cycle of twenty-four hours there is one moment, say for example, every day at 4:44pm, in which there is an expression of Divine wrath and anger?

There is a deeper interpretation to these prophetically inspired words. That when our sages say there is a moment within the day of Divine wrath it means that within every moment there is a moment of wrath, of Gevurah. Within every moment there is a moment of holding back, withdrawing, un-doing. This is the Divine inhale of the life force that just a moment earlier created existence. Within every moment there is the element of Chesed — creating, sustaining, nourishing existence — and an element of Gevurah, destroying and undoing existence. The moment of Gevurah is the time of anger as it were, and when we tap into this 'moment' within the rhythm of time we have the power of Gevurah, to, Heaven forbid, hurt, curse and destroy ourselves and others.

The cosmic Divine exhale is an expression of Chesed - this is our inhale. The Divine inhale is an expression of Gevurah - this is our exhale.

Being that there are these two forces, we, who are created in the Divine Image, are a mirror reflection of reality. And so it is our right against the Divine left, as it were, and our left against the Divine right, our out against the cosmic in, and our in corresponding to the Divine out. In essence, our inhale is drawing in the Divine exhale, the movement outward from the Creator, to create, sustain and nourish reality; this is Divine Chesed. Our exhale moves into the Divine inhale, the Divine Gevurah, a death of sorts.

Every moment we are being reborn and dying — dying in the exhale and being reborn in the inhale.

> •Inhale: "I am alive"
> •Exhale: "I am dying"
> •In the retention, between the two, life flows.

Our life is maintained in the space between the inhale and exhale.

CHESED / OUTWARD COSMIC EXHALE, GEVURAH / INWARD COSMIC INHALE & TIFERES/ THE BALANCE

Our sages tell us, "In beginning there was a Divine thought to create the world with strict judgment, Din and Gevurah, but the Creator observed that that world would not sustain itself, so the Creator joined it with the attribute of Rachamim, kindness and compassion" *(Medrash Rabba)*.

The simple reading of this text is that there is an original thought and than a second guess and an alternative way. On a deeper, more integral level, these two conceptions of creation represent two elements within creation itself.

There is an element of creation that is Din, "strict judgment", within creation, and there is an element of Chesed, "unlimited kindness" within creation, and there is also the balance between the two. Life itself is the perfect giving with the perfect receiving. In truth, it is in the place of the balance and harmony between these two that allows existence to flourish.

The equilibrium between Chesed and Gevurah is not only needed in order to create, but ever since creation — and remember, creation is continuous — there needs to be a balance of forces so that creation continues to exist and is not overwhelmed by the Infinity of the Creator. If there is not any constriction, there is no possibility for a creation to emerge in the first place.

RABBI MENDEL OF VITEBSK (1730-1788)

In the words of an early Chassidic Rebbe, R. Mendel of Vitebsk, a prime disciple of the Maggid of Mezritch, who in turn was the prime disciple of the Baal Shem Tov.

[Excerpted and Translated from the 'Pri Ha'Aretz']

"The world is founded on Chesed, a Divine expansion, as it says, Olam Chesed Yibane, "a world of Chesed He established" (Tehilim, 89:3).

Yet, there can be no creation without the act of Tzimtzum, constriction, withdrawal of the Divine flow, since the Divine flow is Infinite (and there would be no room for finitude, for creation, to emerge). Therefore there must be Gevurah and Din, judgment and constriction.

On the other hand, with Gevurah alone, (once the world was created) the world would not be able to be sustained, since Gevurah is 'withdrawal and lack of expansion'.

As our sages have said, "In the beginning there was a Divine thought to create the world with strict judgment, Din, but the Creator observed that world would not sustain itself thus, so the Creator joined the attribute of Rachamim, kindness and compassion".

The joining together of both Chesed with Gevurah is Rachamim.

Chesed is called 'expansion without limit', as the word Chesed is Chas Dalus, meaning to "fill in the lack" (Tikunei Zohar, Tikkun 22). If this were to be the case – a world in which the Divine expansion fulfills every lack - the world would cease to be as separate existence, and become Unified and filled with the Oneness of the Creator.

Rachamim (the attribute of Tiferes), which is the joining of both the forces (Chesed and Gevurah) in the perfect balance, is the main (force) of creation and that which allows it to exist, and this force is called Tiferes."

(Pri Ha'Aretz. Parshas Vayeshev. p 33-34)

Balance is what is needed to sustain our creation. For this world to exist — to be created and not overwhelmed Infinity, to be able to sense independence and autonomy and yet to still be linked to the Creator through the middle column of Tiferes — compassion is required. Chesed is to give without limitations, thus completely overwhelming and disregarding the vessel of the receiver. Gevurah is to be overly sensitive to the vessels of the receiver, so much so, as to completely withhold from giving all together. Compassion is to give with the appropriate sensitivity of what the receiver is equipped to receive.

Tiferes is the middle column reality — giving without overwhelming, restricting without withholding everything. Our reality is founded on Chesed, created through the act of Gevurah, and sustained by Tiferes. Tiferes allows a reality that senses its independence and yet is, upon reflection, a creation that is easily and eternally linked to its Creator.

Our world is maintained on a three-column structure. As a reflection of this truth the first letter of the Torah is the letter Beis, ב , which is the number two, as it bespeaks of duality, but is configured of three lines or columns. It is the middle column that upholds the tension, maintaining the divergent and conflicting forces of Chesed - giving, extending, outward movement, and Gevurah - contraction, limiting, inward movement - in perfect harmony.

A healthy, physically-balanced person is one with a healthy spine, a person whose middle, centering column is in order. The primary prayer in the daily liturgy is the *Amidah*, the "standing" prayer. Parenthetically, prayer is likened to the spine, as a spiritually healthy person is one who can stand appropriately with a healthy, balanced spine.

ENTERING INTO THE DIVINE FLOW
OF CREATION:
DEEP INHALING & EXHALING

The ever-present oscillation between these two moods of Chesed and Gevurah, expansion and contraction, can be felt within our bodies as we breathe — the contraction as we inhale and expansion as we exhale, and Tiferes is the in between state, the retention.* When we inhale we constrict,

---

*Chesed, Gevurah and Tiferes are inhale, exhale and retention. The root of the teaching that breath is related to our soul, our life force, is from the Medrash on the final verse of Tehilim, "Kol HaNeshama Tehallel, "With all my soul you shall praise." Neshamah, "soul", can be read as the word Neshima, "breath". We can then read the verse from Tehillim as saying, "with every breath a person takes he shall praise G-d". The first letters of these three words Kol HaNeshama Tehallel, are Kof, Hei and Tof, which together spell the Hebrew word Ta'ke. Ta'ke is one of the Seventy-Two Divine names of G-d. In addition, when one takes the Divine name Sha'dai (Shin - Daled –Yud), the following three letters in the Aleph Beis are Tof, (after Shin) Hei (after Dalet) Kof (after Yud), which spell the name Ta'ke. It is the name through which Moshe killed the Egyptian oppressor when he said, Lama Ta'ke, "why are you hitting?" According to our sages he took the life of that Egyptian by reciting a holy name. That name was Ta'ke. These letters have the power to take life. Essentially, it is a name of Gevurah, restriction and harsh judgment. In reverse, the name Ta'ke is derived from the verse, Ve'ahavta Es Hashem Elokecha, "You shall love Hashem your G-d." The final letters of the last three words, Es Hashem Elokecha are Tof, Kof and Hei, which spell Ta'ke. The hitting

there is a contraction of the external intercostal muscles as we draw in air, our diaphragm contracts, tightens, and moves downward. And when we exhale there is an expansion, as we expel the air and relax the external intercostal muscles and release the air outward.

We are a perfect embodiment of the cosmic process of creation when our inhale is viewed as a Tzimtzum, constriction and contraction, an act of Gevurah; and our exhale is seen as releasing and expansion, an act of Chesed. There is a Kabbalistic image of the Creator holding His breath, contracting the Light, which is the act of Tzimtzum. Through this contraction the world was darkened. And then from this darkness the world was revealed, crafted and carved *(R. Shem Tov Ibn Shem Tov. Safer Ha'emunos, Shar 4)*. A deep inhale and holding of breath is a darkening of creation; and an exhale, a letting go of the supernal breath, is a revealing of light. This Tzimtzum and release is continuous, as creation is forever renewed every moment.

---

comes from love. The Ta'ke is rooted in Ve'ahavta, "you shall love." The numeric value of the name Tof-400, Kof -20, and Hei -5, is similar to the total of Mashiach Ben David, as Moshiach is where judgment will be shown through kindness. Neshamah–Neshimah contains both Chesed and Gevurah together. This is the element of Tiferes.

This awareness can be an actual meditative practice, the mimicking of the cosmic creative process. Inhaling as withdrawing inwards and exhaling as an act of creation. In fact, every time we exhale we are releasing energy, creating and shaping the world around us. There are four basic elemental properties: fire, wind, water and earth. Earth essentially is included within the primary three — fire, wind and water *(Pardes Rimonim, 93)*. In general, breath is associated with the element of "fire." The letters of the Hebrew word for "breath", *Hevel*, can be rearranged to spell *L'hav*, a "flame" *(Tikkunei Zohar, Tikkun 21.p. 49b. Siddur Ma'harid, p. 15a)*. Yet, more broadly speaking, breath is harnessing and releasing back into the world the elements of wind and water, as in the moist vapor that is ejected, and fire, as in the heat *(Zohar 11, 238b, Ta'amei HaMitzvos, Radbaz, Mitzvah 112)*.

In this way, the act of exhaling is a glimmer of an actual creation, a revealing and pushing out of the elements into the world.

As an actual meditative practice one would begin by taking deep inhales, bringing the breath all the way down to the tip of the body, holding down the breath for a moment or two, and then releasing the breath in a powerful exhale. One would do so over and over again, —deep inhales and deep exhales — with proper intention and thus consciously enter into the Divine flow of creation, thereby sensing a unity with the Creator.

One can become a little more innovative and add the two sides of the nostrils into the equation. The two orifices of the nose are generally linked with the right and left side of the body — the right nostril is associated with the right column of Chesed and the left nostril with Gevurah. More specifically, as the nose is in the center of the body, the nose as a whole is associated with the middle column. When seen from this perspective, the right nostril is aligned with the attribute of Tiferes and the left with Yesod *(Sefer Yetzirah, 4:7-13)*.

In this paradigm the inhale is the act of drawing inwards, Gevurah, and the exhale is the creative act, Chesed. Applying some pressure on the right nostril, breathe in from the left, Gevurah *(Yesod)* nostril, all the way to the tip of the body. Hold the breath for a moment or two and then breathe out through the right, Chesed *(Tiferes)* nostril, the act of creating. Over time, one would be able to control inhaling from one nostril and exhaling out the other, without needing to use the fingers.

Being a little more creative, one may add another dimension into the mix, and that is the breathing of the ears. The AriZal speaks figuratively about a very thin, subtle and refined breath of the ears. Just as there is breath that comes from the nose, and in a more pronounced and powerful manner, breath that comes from the mouth, the ears also emit some form of breath. The breath of the ears is a higher level of breath, originated from a higher source *(Eitz Chayim, Heichal 2 (Nekudim) Shar 1:1)*. All the orifices of the head emit and release as they gather energy. The eyes, because they represent the highest openings in the body, do not release any vapor or breath. Rather, they radiate lights, transmitting subtle waves that have tangible effects on physical reality. The highest form of breath is therefore from the ears *(Eitz Chayim, Heichal 1 (A'k) Shar 4:1)*.

Did you ever notice that when you cover your ears you hear a faint sound? This, says the AriZal, is the sound of breath or air that is pushing to escape the ear cannel, but is blocked by your hand. The right ear is connected with the right column and the higher persona and the left ear is connected with the left column and the lower persona. As you are alternating left and right nostril, inhaling from the left and exhaling from the right, gently cover the right ear canal as you breathe in, and the left as your breathe out.

In the cosmic creative process, creation emerges into being through speech. The Creator said "Let there be light, and there was light." Breath became wind that became speech, the Divine utterances of creation. The mouth is the instrument of speech and expression. It is the embodiment of Malchus, the lower, center middle column. One, therefore, can also practice breathing in from the nostrils and breathing out from the mouth. The inward movement of the inhale through the nose and the outward movement of the exhale through the mouth, the medium through which speech is revealed.

The below is both a Reflection and a Materialization of the Above. A materialization is where the below and the Above are exactly alike, as it were. The "right side" of the Above is the right side of the below. This is when our inhale is similar to the Divine inhale, an act of Gevurah and Tzimtzum, and our exhale is analogous to the Divine exhale, an act of Chesed. A reflection is where the below is the exact opposite image of the Above. This is when our inhale mirrors the Divine exhale and our exhale mirrors the Divine inhale.

As we inhale, we are also filling ourselves with new life force and renewed energy, filling ourselves with the Divine flow of Chesed. When we exhale, we are letting go of air, releasing our life force, emptying ourselves back into creation, and returning our breath in Gevurah.

The movement of life force, of the Divine flow to create, nurture, nourish, sustain and replenish creation moves in and out of creation continuously. Chesed moving forward, extending outward to create; and then immediately, actually simultaneously, Gevurah retracting and ceasing to create. The cosmic energy flows much like breath does, in and out, back and forth, touch and go, rapidly 'reaching and not reaching'.

THE MAGGID OF MEZRITCH

Here is an original teaching from the Maggid of Mezritch, the primary student of the Baal Shem Tov:

> *[Excerpted and Translated from the 'Ohr HaEmes']*
>
> *"...With every breath we take we shall praise the Creator...the Chayos or "Divine flow" flows into the world in the form of Mati V'lo Mati, "reaching and not reaching", (meaning, the Divine Light enters to create, sustain, and nourish, and then immediately retracts) because the body cannot maintain its existence if there was too great of an influx of Divine plenty, (it would be overwhelmed and thus cease to exists as an apparent separate entity) and also the Divine flow (of spiritual reality) cannot tolerate being enclothed within a form, a body, for too long. Hence, the Divine flow enters the body and then immediately returns Above. This is the breath."*
>
> *(Ohr Ha'emes, Imrei Tzadikim, p 4).*

Divine life force pulsates as breath moving in the form of *Mati V'lo Mati*, "reaching and not reaching", touching and not touching, it is both here and not here. The life force enters us and immediately exits, it is forever slippery and allusive. This rapid back and forth movement is also called *Ratzu V'shuv*, "running and returning". Breath, as the conduit of energy, moves in a pattern of Ratzu V'Shuv.

RATZU V'SHUV/
RUNNING & RETURNING

Ratzu V'Shuv, "running and returning", back and forth is a movement that is found in the mystical vision of Yechezkel, Ezekiel. In his vision he encounters angels that are called Chayos that move in the manner of Ratzu, running, and Shuv, returning. His prophetic experience is channeled through a prism of running and returning.

Experientially, because the Divine life force enters creation in the manner of Ratzu V'Shuv, every time we sense that we are experiencing some form of clarity, some type of parting of the veil, where we sense the Divine in our life, immediately this sensation disappears. The moment we want to take hold of or appreciate the experience, it slips away and fades. The experience seems similar to a flash of lightening, illuminating our darkness, yet, the moment we want to focus our attention on the lightening it vanishes.

As long as we function from a place of duality, where we are 'separate' from the Source of all life, our experiences of that Source will forever be in the form of touch and go, running and returning, touching and not touching. The experience will always be transitory and fleeting, like a flash of lightening the illuminates the night, but just as quickly disappears.

Our physical mode of apparatus — our heartbeat, breath and pulse, as all of life — flows in this same pattern of reaching and not reaching, going and returning. Our inhale is a Divine reaching, a cosmic running as the Divine flow enters and fills us, giving us renewed strength and life; and the exhale is the not reaching, the returning as the Divine flow leaves us and is returning to its Source.

As explored earlier, our movement is the mirror reverse image of the cosmic. Every exhale is a Ratzu, a desire to expire, a death of sorts, a desire to move upward, a running back to our Source. Every inhale is a Shuv, a returning of Divine energy flow, filling bodies, enlivening our souls.

With every exhale our soul takes wing and rushes to join her Beloved, and with every inhale her Beloved sends her back into the body.

Our Ratzu, exhale, is emptied into the Divine Shuv, the Gevurah, inward movement upward. Our Shuv, the return into body, is a breathing in of the Divine Ratzu, the Chesed, energy flow running into and filling creation, moving our souls back into our bodies.

This movement of expiring (exhale) and renewing (inhale) is continuous. Experientially, the movement of Ratzu is the desire to die, to let go, to run back to our Source, to expire as individual separate i. The movement of Shuv, the return of the breath back into the body, is the awareness that our purpose lies within the body, otherwise, we would not be embodied.

OUR DEEPEST RATZU- YEARNING IS FOR COMPLETION

What is our deepest Ratzu? We always yearn for more, maybe a new car, more shoes, another new gadget, but what is the deepest Ratzu? This is our yearning to connect with the Ein Sof, "Infinity".

We all experience a yearning for more. Incompleteness is part of our human condition. Many times, people are convinced that if they get that new car, new pair of shoes, or the newest gadget, they are going to finally feel complete and fulfilled. Because we always feel 'incomplete', we assume these things will bring us completeness. Yet, the deeper reason we feel incomplete is because we are a Creation, hence by definition we are in fact 'incomplete'; we are forever dependent on a Creator that created us. Our completion comes about by the realization that we are incomplete as a creation and that we are connected with our Creator. This is the essence of completion and wholeness.

There is *Shalem*, "wholeness" and completion; and there is Cheser, "incompletion". The Creator is Shalem, complete, and everything that is created is inherently incomplete, Cheser. Part of the nature of creation is this sense of Cheser, incompleteness.

We, creation, all yearn for completion, to become immortal, to wield creator-like power, and to be in full control over our lives. On the deeper level, this is a yearning for our Creator, to be like the Creator, to be complete.

Paradoxically, the only way for a creation, an ontologically incomplete being, to sense completion is by surrendering the very notion of trying to be complete and in full control; and instead, to sense the incompletion and the dependency on the Creator. Humility for what is beyond our total control and gratitude for what we do have links us to our Creator and thus ensures a sense of inner completion and wholeness.

RATZU AS A YEARNING TO EXPIRE & SHUV AS AN AWARENESS OF THE HERE AND NOW

The extreme expression of Ratzu, the impulse to 'run', to let go, to exhale is our Ratzu to expire in ecstasy or at least to ascend the trivialities of this colloquial world. Yet, Shuv is our returning, the deep awareness that the purpose of life is in this world, in the here and now.

In the lower, less evolved stages of spiritual maturity the running is expressed as a desire to transcend the world, while neglecting the body. In the more mature stages, our running energy is in total harmony with its divine purpose, which is to be in the Shuv, vested within the world, while simultaneously inspiring to transform what is. The Baal Shem Tov said that when he was young he refrained from speaking with simple folk so as not to break his spiritual mindset and equilibrium. But as he matured he realized that speaking with others not only did not disturb his spiritual state, but Hashem's presence can and is found in every encounter.

THE UNITY OF RATZU V'SHUV

There is a dynamic interplay between Ratzu and Shuv when seen from a place of Unity, they are not only contradictory, rather they are meant to serve and enhance each other. Running ensures an energetic lightness of being that prevents our involvement with world and body from devolving into self-centered pre-occupation or existential anxiety. Returning ensures that we are grounded, that we do not neglect the body or slip fully into ecstasy and expire from the world.

As mentioned, breathing is a physiological embodiment of the dynamic of running and returning. Each exhale is a desire to run, emptying ourselves and expiring; and each inhale is a desire to 'return' to the body and fill ourselves with new energy. Within every inhale–exhale motion there is also the retention. Between every inhale and exhale, as well as in between every exhale and inhale, there is a moment of retention when we are neither inhaling nor exhaling. This motionless state of retention is beyond the 'running and returning' paradigm, it is the Unity that contains and maintains both. The inhale/exhale structure operates within a level of duality, either moving in or out. The pause, the retention, the stillness is the unity beyond movements. The retention is the middle column, the place of balance.

Both physical and spiritual health and wholeness rests on this balance of running and returning. This is not an either/or question — either living from a place of running or from a place of returning — rather, the purpose is to achieve a balance of running and returning. A resolution needs to be secured between the yearning to expire, which is a desire for transcendence, coupled with a deep awareness of our purpose in the here and now.

Creation and the entire creative process depends on this 'in and out', 'reaching and not reaching', 'running and returning' paradigm. The root of this paradigm is the Torah itself, the blueprint and prototype of creation. In Hebrew, the words רצוא ושוב, Ratzu V'shuv, contain the numeric value of 611. *Ratzu* is 297, *V'Shuv* is 314. 297+314=611. This is the exact same numerical value as the word Torah *(Bris K'hunas Olam, Maamor Shabbos)*. The entire Torah is founded on this principle of running and the returning, striking a balance between spirituality, transcendence, and physical immanence, seeking to bring heaven to earth and even deeper, revealing the unity and oneness between heaven and earth.

MEDITATION III

RATZU V'SHUV

....

RUNNING & RETURNING

....

INHALE-EXHALE-RETENTION
BREATH MEDITATION

HAVING AN AWARENESS AND UNDERSTANDING of the process of Ratzu and Shuv can deepen our experience of conscious breathing. With every exhale, one would focus on their Ratzu, their yearnings and desires, and with every inhale, one would focus on their purpose of life and whether they are living fully and actualizing the deepest reason for being.

In the subtle, motionless pause of the retention, the stillness beyond the movement, it is extremely valuable to maintain a positive thought. In the retention prior to the exhale, ask yourself: "what is my inner most desire and yearning"? Then let out a deep exhaled affirmation. In the retention before the inhale, think a moment: "am I living my purpose, am I living fully, am I articulating who I deeply am?" And then with the inhale draw inwards the answer into your body, psyche and consciousness.

MEDITATION III:
BREATHING
....
Inhale–Exhale–Retention: Running & Returning
....

STEP BY STEP:
....

Every meditation begins with a commitment to honor the time you make for your practice. Clear space on your daily calendar, space in your home, space in yourself. Arrange the physical space to feel as inviting, warm and safe as can be.

....

Sit in your designated meditation spot comfortably, relaxed and fully present. You do not need to close your eyes, but it may be helpful. As the eyes close the chin slightly lowers and the face softens.

....

Take a moment to center yourself in this moment, in this space, the here and now, the only moment there is. As you strengthen your center, the external chaos will dull and, over practice, fade away.

....

You may notice various sounds, sensations, thoughts or feelings arise. Observe it all without changing a thing.

....

Guide your awareness to your breathing. Let the breath flow in and out through the nostrils.

....

If your mind wanders, gently return your awareness to the sensation of the breathing. If you find yourself following your thoughts, return your awareness to the groundedness of your seat. As you hold center, thoughts can come and go as easily as clouds move throughout the sky.

....

On the exhalation, think about your deepest Ratzu/ running: What are your aspirations? Is your yearning on the physical level: fame, money, power? Is your yearning on the spiritual level: connection, transcendence, something greater?

....

Meditate on the deep yearning to be an integrated whole, the satisfaction that comes in the wake of shedding external forms, titles, possessions.

....

On the inhalation, think about your deepest Shuv/ returning. Do you have a clear awareness of your purpose in this world? Are you in touch with what you need to do in order to embody your full potential?

....

Draw your awareness to the retention between inhaling and the exhaling. At the top of the inhalation, when your lungs are full, summon a positive thought, e.g., "My deepest yearning is for transcendence." Make a mental affirmation that although you may be busy throughout the day securing financial stabilities, your deepest yearning is to connect with the Creator, to bring transcendence into your life. Exhale.

At the bottom of the exhalation, when the lungs are empty, summon a positive thought, e.g., "I will search and I will find my purpose in life." Mentally affirm that although you may be busy making ends meet, you will begin to be more attentive to the reality you are in, to look for and find purpose in everything in your life, from parents, siblings, spouse, children, friends, co-workers, to the place you find yourself living, to the body you possess.

Sit with the awareness that your soul embodied into this world for a one-of-a-kind reason and a distinct Tikkun/correction. There is something that you, and only you, can contribute to the universe. In this retention period, allow your mind to be filled with a positive thought; "I am charged with my sense of mission."

Seal your practice with this genuine devotion for living purposefully. Let the presence of Shuv invigorate your body.

BREATH

....

MOVING FROM FEAR, TO AWE, TO PLEASURE

....

Every exhale is essentially a glimmer of our final exhale, a miniature form of death. We begin life with an inhale and end life with an exhale.

We refresh with every inhale and expire with every exhale.

When we simply pay attention to our breath, especially to our outbreaths, it can actually be at first quite frightening. As you are exhaling you are emptying yourself, letting go, dying a little bit. The first immediate sensation that may arise when thinking about our exhales and realizing that we are dying a little, is fear.

Fear sets in whenever we sense that our ego is in real or assumed danger. Fear is a phenomenon of the ego. That is, the ego fear its own annihilation and termination. The greatest fear is the fear of death, the fear the ego has of no longer existing.

Fear is a by-product of the ego and its dire need to self-perpetuate. Observing our exhale, our dying a little bit, our surrendering, can, from the lens of the ego, be quite frightening. As we are tenaciously bound with our ego, a tension arises with the realization of the transient nature of the ego and that it may no longer serve a purpose.

The deeper and more aware of the outbreaths one becomes, slowly the fear subsides and an overwhelming sense of awe sets it. Fear functions when one is still desperately clinging to the ego and not willing to give up the small i in the face of the vastness of reality. When one lives from the place of the small i, the ego is confined within a very small place. There is the "you", with your genetics and life story, that stands in contrast and often in battle with the entire world around you. Life from the place of ego is very small. With every exhale the small i is expiring, emptying itself into the vastness, the mystery of the "everything". Fear moves to awe when one senses the beauty of letting go of the small i. The moment one lets go, they slip into the majesty of creation and the fullness of the Big I of the Creator.

One becomes more by being less.

PLEASURE & LETTING GO OF ASSUMED CONTROL

In the exhale, as in the inevitability of death, we let go, we relinquish control, and that is what makes the fear ever more acute. We walk through life thinking we have full control over our lives and destiny. But whenever we feel like we are losing control, fear grips us. Do we really have full control over the circumstances of our lives? Sure, our responses are always within our control. But the externalities (e.g. whether the flight goes well, or G-d forbid, there are some difficulties) are beyond our control. The illusion that somehow we can still control every situation is the root of so much of our fear.

In truth, there is a controller, but it is not you alone. There is the Creator, the Master of the Universe who is in control. The deeper we go, the more completely the fear dissipates and melts into awe, surrender, and letting go.

In awe we take leave of our ego. Any form of awe is to lose oneself in something or someone greater or larger than oneself. At the moment of awe there is very little self that is involved, certainly there is no self- awareness. Being awe-struck we momentarily lose our ego and sense of self. We become one with that which inspired the awe.

This taking leave of the ego, wherein we let go of our assumed control and recognize the Ultimate controller, moves us from awe to Ta'anug, "pleasure", spiritual bliss and elation.

A deeper paradox is that not only do we become more by being less, but the deeper the Ta'anug the less consciously we experience it. The higher and more profound the pleasure, the 'less' one is present and aware of themselves experiencing that pleasure. By contrast, the more present one is in the experience, the more separate one is from the experience and thus the less pleasurable. Spiritual pleasure works the same way and, in fact, it is the meta-root of all pleasure. Spiritual delight and pleasure arise from a place of awe. First one experiences an overwhelming sense of awe, a loss of oneself and one's ego, which organically morphs into a tremendous measure of pleasure, bliss and ecstasy.

In the exhale we die a little bit and our consciousness moves from fear to awe to pleasure. The more powerful the exhale — the more we die, let go, and surrender — the quicker and deeper we move through the stages of fear, awe and pleasure. Pleasure is still a 'sensation', a feeling. There is still some measure of i. Eventually, pleasure slips into unity, into Ayin, no-thing-ness, and the i dissolves within what is pleasurable, within, in this context, the Divine I.

In the process of creating new life two separate beings merge as *Basar Echad*, "one flesh" *(Bereishis, 2:24)* in unity, so that a third can be birthed. The male, the inseminator, who exhales and expunges all his energy and life force, actually involuntarily pauses from breathing at the moment of unity *(Likutei MaHaran, 60:3)*. In this pausing from breath, he symbolically dies, as it is a stage beyond the exhale, the final breath. The pause is what comes after the fear that has become awe that has morphed into pleasure. It is the total Ayin, "no-thing-ness", and thus it is the space in which new Yesh, new life can emerge. Being Ayin one becomes the vehicle and medium through which the Ein Sof, the Infinite Light of the Creator, can manifest. Creating children, the infinite perpetuation of our kind, is a revealed expression of the Ein Sof power within the finite world. When we are Ayin, no-thing, empty, unified, the Ein Sof can become revealed.

NOTHING HIGHER THAN PLEASURE

"There is nothing higher than *Oneg*, "pleasure", and nothing lower then *Nega*, "psycho-physical ritual impurity due to skin discoloration" *(Safer Yetzirah)*. The words Oneg and Nega share the same letters, the same spiritual DNA, in variant order.

Oneg is pleasure, which is a dynamic of unity, of *Yichud*. Nega is symbolic of separation. The metaphysical root of why a person would suffer with this spiritual malady is *Lashon Harah* or "negative speech". Nega is triggered by people speaking ill of others thus causing separation between people *(Erchin, 15b)*. One who speaks negatively about others is punished with a Nega, a skin discoloration, and the law of a person with a Nega is that they need to sit alone, outside the community in isolation.

The purpose of this separation is for them to realize the pain of separation that they caused by their actions. In other words, they are to do the inner work of *Tikkun*, "rectification" and repair, and thus be spiritually, emotionally, mentally and eventually physically healed.

Pleasure is unity. The more unity, the more pleasure. This is the reason why the deepest pleasure in the world is the pleasure of being one with Hashem, with the Creator. Everything else pleasurable is a mere glimpse of the ultimate pleasure *(Berachos, 57b)*. Any earth-bound pleasure by definition still labors under the burdens of duality. There is still always me, you, object or subject. Only with the true Ayin, the Ein Sof, the Infinite Light of the Creator, which is empty of all form and dimension, can we truly experience the deepest highest level of unity — losing our I within the Ayin of the Ein Sof.

Essentially, every exhale moves us through these three stages, and beyond. What begins as fear moves into awe, a joyful letting go, emptying oneself, and then, the less we are the more pleasure sets in. The awe leads into pure pleasure and bliss, losing oneself in the presence of the Ultimate.

MEDITATION IV

BREATHING

FROM FEAR, TO AWE,

TO PLEASURE

MEDITATION IV:

BREATHING

From Fear, to Awe, to Pleasure

STEP BY STEP:

Every meditation begins with a commitment to honor the time you make for your practice. Clear space on your daily calendar, space in your home, space in yourself. Arrange the physical space to feel as inviting, warm and safe as can be.

Sit in your designated meditation spot comfortably, relaxed and fully present. You do not need to close your eyes, but it may be helpful. As the eyes close the chin slightly lowers and the face softens.

Take a moment to center yourself in this moment, in this space, the here and now, the only moment there is. As you strengthen your center, the external chaos will dull and, over practice, fade away.

Guide your awareness to your breath, in and out

through the nostrils, soft, quiet and steady.

If your mind wanders, gently return your awareness to the sensation of the breathing. If you find
yourself following your thoughts, let go of them,
and return to your breath. Keep on going back to
your breath until the mind settled on the breath.

Begin to focus your attention on your out-breaths.

Encouraging the breath to grow deeper, allow the
exhalation to be experienced throughout your
entire body. As you exhale, your abdomen draws
back, shoulders roll forward and head lowers
down.

The emptiness which comes with exhalation is a
death. If the sensation of fear sets in at this point,
that is alright; the ego is rising. Right now before
you is the opportunity to recognize the root of
this fear as the fear of relinquishing control you
have assumed yours.

Relinquish control. Allow the exhalation to literally deflate your torso, entering an internally-fo-
cused forward fold. When you have visited the
bottom of this emptiness, after multiple cycles of

breath, slowly rise anew on an inhalation.

....

Repeat this body-breath movement many times,
each time exploring further. As fear melts, Divine
Awe is born and you can witness the vastness of
the universe, the awesomeness of creation and
Creator.

....

Sit with this awe and allow it to reveal a great
pleasure of being one with the Source of all life,
a type of spiritual bliss of being one.

....

Seal your practice from within the embrace of
this Divine bliss.

....

BREATH AS RENEWAL & REBIRTH

Every Moment is New

Every moment we are dying and being rebirthed; dying in the exhale, being reborn in the inhale.

Every moment there is a renewed *Ko'ach Ha-Hischadshus*, "power of renewal", that is being breathed into creation. Creation is continuous. Every moment creation is being manifest from Ayin, a state of non-being, into a Yesh, an existent state of being.

Creation is *Yesh M'Ayin*, "something from no-thing", Ex Nihilo *(Ramban, Abarbanel, Bereishis, 1:1. Medrash HaGadal, Ibid)*. Prior to the world being revealed there was only Infinity — formless and unmanifest. From our Yesh perspective — a solidified reality operating in a time/space continuum where we contextualize and quantify everyone and every-thing — what created us is considered as Ayin. We refer to the Infinite and unmanifest as Ayin because from our per-spective Infinity is intangible, it is no-thing. We call what is Above Ayin because the Creator is beyond our comprehen-sion *(Shaarei Orah. Shar 5. Shar 9. Pardes Rimonim, Shar 23:1)*. The Creator is beyond all definition; beyond even the definition of being beyond definition *(Tanya, Shar HaYichud VeHaEmunah, 9. Mifalos Elokim 2;5. Nefesh HaChayim, 1:13, note)* Quite simply, a "some-thing" cannot ever grasp the "Every-thing."

As mentioned, our realty is Yesh and the Above is Ayin. We call creation Yesh M'ayin, something from no-thing, but this creation is not a one-time only event in the past. Rather, creation is an ever-unfolding process. Every moment Yesh is being created from/by Ayin.

As everyone and everything is being born, reborn and created at this very moment, nothing is truly old, stale, or even predicable. The present is a truly new moment, with new opportunity.

All of Creation is being created out of no-thing-ness continuously and at this very moment. Because of the continuous renewal of every moment we can begin again, we can press the reset button at any time.

THE POSSIBILITY TO RESTART AT ANY MOMENT

If creation was set into motion at the beginning of creation than the laws of cause and effect dictate that everything that flows from that moment is predictable and inevitable. If creation is not continuous, than that which occurred in our past inevitably informs the present and imprints our future. We would forever be trapped by the doings or not-doings of our past, which are also at the mercy of a pervious past, including the actions of our parents, and our parents' parents, all the way back to the first point of creation.

If there were no way to unshackle ourselves from our past we would forever be crushed by the burden of our errors. Without the power to disengage we might as well resign ourselves to a hamster wheel of inevitability and relentless motion without any real advancement.

However, because of the *ko'ach ha-hischadshus*, "power of renewal", there is always the possibility to restart. Every moment is completely new and loaded with potential.

We ought to never feel despondent, hopeless or dispirited because of our past doing. Nothing of the past can hold us hostage. We ought to behold the very moment we are in as it truly is — a fresh new moment. As Rabbeinu Yonah of Gerona, the 13th century Catalan sage writes: "The foundation for genuine change is to consider today as the day you were born, the first day of your life, and you have no faults or merits" *(Yesod Ha'teshuvah)*.

When we observe the moment as it truly is, we can begin anew right now.

And being as it is a new beginning, we have the ability to release ourselves from the imprints of the past and untangle ourselves from our automatic, preprogrammed responses. What is more, by letting go of the person we thought we were, we can become the person we truly are.

One of the Hebrew words for "sin" is *Aveira*. Aveira has the same root as the Hebrew word for "past", *Avar*. Sin sometimes suggests a kind of holding on to past that is no longer present. Whether it means being crushed by the burdens of one's past mistakes and feeling that you can never be a good person because of those actions; or even more deeply, feeling like, "I am who I am and I can never change". This way of thinking is a sin. True, our actions have consequences. Yet, a person can confidently affirm, "I am not a slave to my past. The Creator is continually creating the world anew every moment. I can tap into this power of renewal and begin again right now".

RABBI LEVI YITZCHAK OF BARDITCHAV

Rabbi Levi Yitzchak of Barditchav was a celebrated student of the Maggid of Mezritch, who in turn, was the prime disciple of the Baal Shem Tov. The book he authored is called *Kedushas Levi*, "The Sanctity of Levi".

[Excerpted and Translated from the 'Kedushas Levi']

"(The word) Now refers to Teshuvah, "personal transformation". The reason why now is equated with transformation is because every single one of Israel is obliged to believe with complete faith that every single moment he is receiving new life force from the Creator. Our sages have taught on the verse, "All

of one's soul shall praise G-d". This means that with every breath a person takes he should offer praise. Because every moment…the Creator sends forth a new life force…since he believes that right now he is a new creation his desire to change at this very moment is effective."

(Kedushas Levi, Megilas Eicha)

A CONTINUALLY RENEWED RELATIONSHIP

The perception of the renewal of creation does wonders for our relationship with the Creator. When we understand how creation emerges every moment anew, moving from Ayin into Yesh, our relationship with the Creator is forever fresh, passionate and renewed. The relationship never feels stale, old or jaded, as G-d is a living presence.

When we look at ourselves and only observe the Yesh — our created existence, i.e. egos and bodies — unrelated to an Ayin — a divine creating, animating force that continuously creates — we are then trapped in the world of routine. Accordingly our relationship with our Creator becomes old, stale and routine. We are then only able to conceive of a Creator who once long ago cared enough, as it were, to create us, but not anymore, G-d is no longer a Living Presence in our life.

[Excerpted and Translated from the 'Kedushas Levi']

"The Creator is present tense. Every moment G-d creates. Every moment the Divine emanates life to all of life. Everything is from Him. He is complete. He includes everything. Therefore, when one experiences a place of Ayin and knows that he is Ayin, for the Creator continuously gives him life, strength and vitality, then he calls the Creator, "Creator", in the present tense; for he knows that right now he is being created. However, when a person observes (only) himself and does not meditate on the Ayin, than indeed he is on the level of Yesh (separate, assumed independent existence) and then he calls the Creator, "the Creator", in the past tense; for he relates to Hashem as He who created him in the past."

(Kedushas Levi, Bereishis)

Life moves continually from Ayin to Yesh. There is never a moment of repetition, inevitability or predictability. Every moment is fresh. Because of this, nothing in our spiritual lives should be performed in an automatic or routine manner. Our relationship with the Creator should always feel as it truly is — a real *Chiddush*, "novelty", something that is constantly fresh and new.

RABBI SCHNEUR ZALMAN OF LIADI

How does one awaken to or become more conscious of this newness? The Alter Rebbe, Rabbi Schneur Zalman of Liadi, a main disciple of the Maggid of Mezritch, writes that not only are we to intellectually contemplate the Yesh M'ayin creative process, but we also need to use our power of imagination.

[Excerpted and Translated from the 'Tanya, Iggeres HaKodesh, 11']

"This means that the creation of Yesh (existence) out of a state of Ayin (no-thing-ness)...occurs every moment...A person should contemplate in the depths of his understanding, and moreover, "picture in his mind", how he comes into being Ex Nihilo at every single moment."

(Tanya, Iggeres HaKodesh, 11)

The Alter Rebbe wants a person to go beyond just thinking about this idea and to picture this process in their mind. Take the information about the creative continuous unfolding and visualize it, make it real. How does one do this?

One simple way is through meditating, thinking and being aware of our breath. For a person who is in a depressed state and finds himself in a funk, in order to feel renewed, recreated and fresh, he should think for a moment or two about the way he breathes. He should take a deep inhale and recognize the radical renewal of energy at this very moment.

[Excerpted and Translated from the 'Kedushas Levi']

"For a person needs to continually ponder and think about how each moment the Creator, in His infinite kindness and compassion, gives him new life, and how every moment the Creator renews him. For this is what it says: "All the Neshmah, "soul"...with every Neshimah, "breath", a person takes one shall praise G-d." Because at every moment the soul desires to leave and expire from the body, and the Creator in His infinite compassion does not allow the soul to leave. Thus, when a person continuously thinks about this idea, (he becomes aware that) every moment is a new creation. This adds passion and excitement to his divine service."

(Kedushas Levi, Rosh Hashanah)

What appears clear from the above teaching is that Reb Levi Yitzchak is encouraging one to think continually about and meditate on the idea of renewal each moment. This is related to thinking about how the soul yearns to expire from the body and how this mechanism is intricately connected with breath.

Every exile is essentially a reflection of a deep Ratzu, yearning to expire, and yet, a moment later, we naturally and involuntarily take in another inhale. This organic flow of out-breath and then immediately in-breath is the way the Creator ensures that our soul does not expire and our *Neshamah* — soul, spirit, life force — which is connected with our *Neshimah*, breath, reenters our body immediately following an exhale.

A simple breathing awareness meditation allows us to deepen our awareness of continuous creation. With every exhalation we are emptying ourselves of our old Yesh, our old state of being; and with every inhalation, we are filling ourselves with new Yesh from the unmanifest Source, the Ayin. This is an act of recreation.

Observing our breath allows us to sense this truth of continuous creation within our bodies. This than, heightens our creativity and reveals the beautiful possibility of beginning anew, right now.

EMPTYING ONESELF INTO THE UNIVERSE

Besides the rebirth and renewal of each moment, each moment is also a moment of death. There is a dying of the old, a letting go of the past. Everything of who you are at the present moment is released and emptied into the universe with every exhale. All your thoughts, words, and actions are imprinted upon your breath as they are exhaled into your surroundings.

Every moment we are completely emptying ourselves, and our deepest innards, into the universe. In the words of the Maggid of Mezritch;

[Excerpted and Translated from the 'Ohr Emes']

"…everything a person speaks and even thinks are imprinted on his breath and when the life force (which is in the breath) returns Above (in the outbreath), all this (thoughts, words and actions) becomes revealed Above…thus a person is judged every moment. A person should be embarrassed to think or do things of folly because everything (all thoughts, words, and actions) moves with one's breath, and this particular thought or action travels Above through all worlds (i.e. whatever you think, speak or do is revealed in all worlds)."

(Ohr Emes, 4).

All of our thoughts, words and actions are emptied and discharged into the universe and travel through all inner worlds, reaching all the way Above. Everything we do, speak or think is revealed and has an effect on the entire cosmos. Not only should be mindful and careful of the actions we do, but even the words we utter and the thoughts we inwardly entertain have a tangible influence on the spiritual equilibrium of the entire world. What occurs on the inside is projected onto the outside and thus has a real effect.

THOUGHTS HAVE AN EFFECT

A person may think to himself: I understand that I should not perpetuate negative actions and I cannot physically hurt someone else. I even understand that I should not speak negativity, even if the person does not hear, as it has an effect on the listeners. But who cares if I amuse myself with negative thoughts about another person? These are thoughts that are only within me. The truth is that even thoughts are revealed and discharged into the environment. If we have positive thoughts we release positive energy into the universe. And if we have negative thoughts we emit toxic energy into the world.

From the great Chassidic master of Dinov:

> *"A person should continuously think how the life force that enters him, enters in the form of Ratzu V'Shuv, "back and forth". This we can clearly see, as breath enters and exits the body continually. Therefore, with our outbreaths all our thoughts ascend upward (inward) to the Creator. Pondering this, one ought to be ashamed of himself, thinking, how all his silly*

thoughts reverberate throughout all worlds…"

(Hanhagas Bnei Yisachar, Takanos Tamchin D'Oraisa)

Everything is interlinked. Our actions in one part of the world have an effect across the globe and alter the very fabric of our reality. Not only on the physical plane, but also on all worlds; and not only actions, but even thoughts and words. Maimonides, the Rambam, writes: "One should see the world, and see himself, as a scale with an equal balance of good and evil. When he does one good deed the scale is tipped to the good, and he and the world is saved. When he does one evil deed, the scale is tipped to the bad, and he and the world is destroyed." *(Hilchos Teshuvah, 3:4. Kidushin, 40b).*

Nothing happens in a vacuum. Our actions, words and thoughts are continually being exhaled into the world, and in reverse, we are continually inhaling other peoples' thoughts, words and actions. Choosing who we wish to surround ourselves with, the community and friends we spend time with, is not only important on a conscious and revealed level, but also incredibly important on a subliminal, subtle energetic level, as we are continually imbibing other people's energy.

Being in the presence of good and righteous people inspires goodness, and conversely, being around negative people, even if they are not doing or even speaking negativity but only having negative thoughts, causes negativity within others.

Some people are more receptive to absorb energy than others. Some are more effected and some less. But every person, on some level, takes in/on other people's energy. The mere act of breathing in, of inhaling, is an absorption of the energy of the other person who has just exhaled himself into one's space.

This is another worthy reason why people should literally surround themselves with good people and stay away from negative people. Besides learning from them, their energy is contagious and infectious as we breathe it in on a subconscious level.

CLOUD OF GLORY

Two or more people who are sitting together and exhaling their positivity create a container of positivity and holiness. Certainly this is true when they do so intentionally, as in a shared meditative experience. But this is also the case when done naturally, without intention.

There was a Cloud of Glory that protected the nation of Israel as they journeyed through the desert. This cloud of holiness and protection, says the Rebbe of Rushin, was created by the collective exhale of the people of Israel themselves. Their shared, yet, multiple breaths morphed into a collective vapor that surrounded and protected them.

GIVING OVER OUR PROBLEMS TO THE CREATOR

On the one hand, the notion that we are emptying ourselves into the world around us demands that we become ever more mindful and cautious, even with regards to the thoughts we have. And yet, from another vantage point, we come to the realization that all of our thoughts, words and actions are in fact emptied into the One Above. With every outbreath we are emptying ourselves into the Creator, as it were.

Every moment is also a time to give up, let go, return, and give over all our hardship and difficulty to the One Above. All thoughts, words and actions are impressed into our outbreath. Our entirety is imprinted within our exhale, and with that breath we are returning everything back to the Source Above. For this reason, exhaling is a time to offer up all our pain, struggle, anxiety, fear, tension, sadness, and worry, everything that is pulling us down, to G-d.

THREE-PRONG PRACTICE

Practically, all of the above can turn into a three-prong breath awareness meditation practice. There is the retention pause between every inhale or exhale and the awareness that one ought to have during this break. There is the actual inhaling and exhaling and the awareness one ought to secure while inhaling and exhaling.

During the inhale one meditates on breathing in as renewal — breathing in from the Divine Ayin into a new potential, a new Yesh. Think about what it means to restart your system, to start all over again, to feel like today is your first day on earth. And during the exhale one contemplates the emptying and returning of our entire existential reality back to the Divine Ayin Above. As you exhale, concentrate on expiring and expunging from within you all toxins, trappings, and definitions, returning everything imprinted upon your breath to the Supernal Breath Above. The exhale is a time to push out and get rid of all negativity.*

The space of the retention is of most value. When you retain your breath before the inhale, entertain a holy, productive thought. Think about how your entire life is from the

_____

*The AriZal speaks about how through the blowing of the Shofar, a "rams' horn", on Rosh Hashanah all Din, "judgment", constrictions and concealments are blown apart and ripped asunder. The act of blowing out opens all blockages and sweetens all strict judgments. Hevel, "breath", in numerical value is 37. There are seven aspects of breath. 37 x 7 = 259 (with 1 added for the word itself, this equals 260). These are the 260 Lights that are revealed when blowing the Shofar.

Creator and is renewed at every moment. And in the retention before the exhale, think about emptying all negativity, everything that is holding you down and blocking you from growth, return it all to the One Above.

MEDITATION V:

BREATHING

....

Renewal at Every Moment

....

STEP BY STEP:

....

Every meditation begins with a commitment to honor the time you make for your practice. Clear space on your daily calendar, space in your home, space in yourself. Arrange the physical space to feel as inviting, warm and safe as can be.

....

Sit in your designated meditation spot comfortably, relaxed and fully present. You do not need to close your eyes, but it may be helpful. As your eyes close the chin slightly lowers and the face softens.

....

Take a moment for letting go of all the internal noise, chaos and movement. Simply be.

....

You may notice various sounds, sensations, thoughts or feelings arise. Observe it all without changing a thing.

....

Guide your awareness to your breathing. Let the breath flow in and out through the nostrils.

If your mind wanders, gently return your awareness to the sensation of the breathing. If you find yourself following your thoughts, allow the thoughts to effortlessly drift away like clouds while you hold this steady space, your center. Keep focus on your breath as the mind settles.

Draw your awareness to the retention between inhalation and exhalation. This momentary pause between each segment of the breath is Ayin, refreshingly still. It is the nothingness of pure potentiality.

The exhalation is the return of this individual breath – and everything that is now imprinted upon the breath - to its source in the Supernal Breath. All of it is absorbed back from where it came. What was received from Above is now given back from below.

As you exhale, let this serve as your meditation: I let go, and expunge from myself all which is negative, all which is small in importance, all which holds me back. I cleanse myself of all negative thoughts that I have thought, spoken or acted upon. In their exit, negativity dies.

As you inhale, let this serve as your meditation: I invite into myself the breath of life, rooted in the Source of all life. Open to the awesomeness of becoming, in this very moment, a Beriah Chada-sha Mamash, a literal new creation, new you with new potential and new beginning.

Sit with this awareness for a few moments.

Seal your practice with the power of full engage-ment and the pledge to be proactive.

MEDITATION VI

BREATHING TECHNIQUE

For Every Day Living

PRACTICAL DAILY APPLICATION

THE ABOVE TEACHINGS AND PRACTICES FROM the Baal Shem Tov and his students were used within a particular context with a specific goal intended, and that was for the purpose of sensing and losing oneself in the unity of the Creator, letting go of negativity, or starting over again. At their core these profound ideas are applicable to various situations in life. Basic breathing techniques, observing the inhale and exhale, and the interconnectivity between everything around and Above us, is a good centering and calming technique that is helpful in many different arenas of life.

You may feel out of focus, scattered, and pulled into various directions, anxiety ridden, filled with fear and cynicism, or overcome by desires and bottomless appetites. These are all good reasons to practice a little bit of basic awareness breathing.

This you can do in the middle of the day, or even while walking down the street. Simply, center yourself for a few moments and take a few conscious mindful breaths.

MEDITATION VI:

BREATHING TECHINQUE

For Every Day Living

STEP BY STEP:

At any given moment throughout the day, when-ever you feel the need for sharpened focus, greater groundedness and the release of inner tension. This meditation practice will serve you.

Stop all activity in this moment right here, right now and take a comfortable seat, relaxed and fully present. You do not need to close your eyes, but it may be helpful. As your eyes close the chin slightly lowers and the face softens.

Center yourself in this moment, in this space, the here and now, the only moment there is. As you strengthen your center, the external distractions will fade and your inner awareness will heighten.

If your mind chases after fleeting thoughts, lov-ingly guide your awareness to the sensation of the breathing. Exhalations draw your torso inwards towards center and inhalations expand your ribcage in all directions.

....

Combine the physical experience of breathing with this meditation: Exhalations cleanse you of what has been and does no longer serve, and inhalations rejuvenate you with fresh vitality and potentiality.

....

Open to center and ground yourself from within the vibrant cycle of breathing.

....

Seal your practice from your deep, grounded core, ever steady and always accessible.

....

PART THREE

BREATHING
&
THE RHYTHM OF
THE PULSE

Our breathing is connected to our heartbeat and thus to our pulse. A pulse is a throbbing of our arteries as blood is pumped from our heart. When we inhale our diaphragm contracts, our lungs expand, and air is sucked in through our nose or mouth. The air then travels down the windpipe into our lungs. Eventually, the oxygen-rich blood from the lungs is delivered to the left side of the heart. The left side of the heart then pumps the blood to the rest of the body. The heart pumps into the body freshly oxygenated blood.

Our exhale is where we eject air rich in carbon dioxide through our nose or mouth.

The pulse reflects outwardly what is occurring inside the body. The health of the body is revealed in the pulse. It is possible to discover within the rhythm, velocity, and spacing of the pulse what is the state of wellbeing of the body. Body and soul mirror each other. It is told that the AriZal was able to discern and diagnose maladies of the soul by feeling a person's pulse *(Shar Ruach HaKodesh, 3. See also: Eitz Chayim, Shar 20;5).*

On the physical plane, to detect a physical ailment by reading a person's pulse, one needs to reach a deep level of concentration so that when they are feeling a pulse, the beating sound fills their entire world of sensation, and every subtle vibration is felt very clearly. This takes a lot of training and sensitivity. All the more so, in order to detect an ailment on a spiritual plane through the rhythm of the pulse demands a tremendous amount of spiritual training and inner work.

A pulse is a recurring pattern of beats. These beats oscillate in intensity and in spacing. Overall, there are ten variations of beats, ten pulses. These ten beats, or 10 lines and dots, corresponds to the ten (nine) Hebrew vowels that give sound and voice to the letters *(Note; Tikunei Zohar, Tikkun 69).*

Each of the vowels has a particular shape. Essentially, they are all comprised of dots and lines, which are reflected in the rhythm and spacing of the beats of the pulse.

These ten vowels in turn correspond to the Ten Sefiros, and more specifically the ten Sefiros within the attribute of Chochmah, wisdom and higher intuition.

Here is a list of the vowels and their correlating Sefiros & their Shape:

1. Kametz (aw) **т** *Keser, deep desire & primordial will*
2. Patach (ah) **‒** *Chochmah, wisdom and intuition*
3. Tzeirei (ei) **••** *Binah, reason and cognition*
4. Segol (eh) **•••** *Chesed, kindness and love*
5. Sh'va (uh) **•** *Gevurah, strength and boundaries*
6. Cholam (oy) **ן** *Tiferes, beauty and compassion*
7. Chirik (ee) **•** *Netzach, victory and perseverance*

8. Kubutz **.**   (U- vowel under the letter)
                         Hod, splendor and humility
9. Shuruk **֫ו**   (U—vowel on top of the letter)
                         Yesod, foundation and relationship
10. No vowels (silence)
                         Malchus, kingship and receptiveness

The beats of the pulse mirror the energy of the Sefiros and Vowels, representing the character of the life force and energy that is most present at this specific time. For example, if a person has a single beat and following that another single beat slightly off to the side, this is a Tzeirei beat; meaning that a person is functioning from an imbalanced place of Binah, "cerebral understanding" and that there is a spiritual/mental/emotional malady in his Binah. And if, for example, a person has a long extended singular beat with a short accompanying one, these together represent the vowel of Kametz and the sefirah of Keser; meaning that a person has an imbalanced strong will and desire and that there is a spiritual/mental/emotional malady in his Keser.

The more dominant the Sefira the more this indicates that there is a blemish because of ones actions in that particular Sefira or in that area of life. Nature generally dictates that if something or someone is in a weakened state, they will gather together all their strength and fight even harder to survive knowing that they are dying.

Observe a flame right before it extinguishes, or a terminally ill person days or moments before they pass on. The sefira that was blemished and weakened fights even harder to survive and thus shows up as most dominant.

This can also be true in the opposite manner. Sometimes the reason that one of the Sefiros or vowels is most dominant is because of a particular Mitzvah, "good deed", that was done, which is energetically aligned with that particular sefira and vowel.

Because of the heightened spiritual sensitivity needed to discern the Kabbalistic cause of a perceived imbalance within someone's pulse, one should not indulge in this practice unguided.

It is for this reason that the above was explained, but not explored in greater detail.

"Instruct the wise and they will be wiser still; teach the righteous and they will add to their learning" *(Mishlei, 9:9).*

A FEW POINTS ABOUT PRACTICING MEDITATION:

THE BEAUTY OF THE PRACTICES THAT WERE explored throughout this text is that they are simple and straightforward. Anyone with even a meager knowledge of Torah or Kabbalah can easily enter into them and begin to practice.

Another wonderful advantage of these techniques is that one can practice them anytime. One can create a set time, say, every morning upon awaking, before the morning prayers or every evening; but one can also use anyone of these methods when simply walking down the street. If you find your mind wandering as you are out walking, practice Hashkata. Or if you feel the need to recharge and reenergize take notice of your breath.

TIME & SPACE

The best method is to set a specific time and a dedicate place when and where your practice will occur. This way, when the time comes and one enters the dedicated space, there is an automatic association with the advantages that comes with the meditation and the mind/body responds accordingly.

If you can choose the time, choose wisely. Seek the right time to meditate; this being whenever you feel least tired and most energetic. This is usually determined by the constraints of your schedule and the availability of your energy. Use your common sense. The length of time dedicated is not the determining factor to the success of the practice. It could be five minutes or five hours. The objective is to dedicate this time completely to the meditation and to be consistent, practicing every day with regularity and consistency.

Meditation is a process that is incompatible with disturbances or interruptions. It requires 100% presence. Take this into consideration when you reserve a specific location for your practice. Make it your space by familiarizing yourself with it and establishing it as a place in which you feel safe and comfortable. Remember, it is okay to change your location if this place does not work for you. If you realize that the spot you have chosen does not optimally serve your practice, find a new spot.

BODY POSITION

The needs of the body must be attended to. It is important that you mediate in a comfortable position. Otherwise your body will let you know that the experience isn't optimal. If you are sitting on the ground and you are not used to doing so, all you will be thinking about is a chair. When you really need a chair, all you can think of is a chair.

Paramount to the style in which you sit is that you are alert with an ease of comfort. There is a fine balance between being comfortable and crossing the line into sluggishness or hyper-relaxation that leads to sleep. Many find that sitting upright is the best position. When we sit up, the mind and body both remain more alert. Sit comfortably erect, in a balanced position. Support the natural curves of the back. Try not to lean too far forward or backwards. Discover your seat.

Of course, if you are walking down the street, none of the above applies.

BEFORE OR AFTER EATING

When you are physically uncomfortable, all you can think about is getting your body into a more comfortable position. The same is true with food. When you are hungry all you can think about is food. Hunger pangs during meditation can cause considerable distraction. Prior to eating, our sages tell us that a person is possessed of two hearts/minds *(Baba Basra, 12b)*. A hungry person cannot think clearly or focus properly.

Conversely, eating a heavy meal beforehand may cause bodily discomfort of another sort, also hindering the meditative experience.

We need to do our best in creating the proper environment and context for our meditation.

BE PATIENT & KIND

"All beginnings are difficult" *(Mechilta. See Rashi, Shemos,19:5. Zohar 11, p. 187)*. If this is something new, it is going to come with some challenge. We need to be patient and kind with ourselves.

It is on us to remember that although starting a new practice can seem awkward and uphill, it gets easier with time and consistency, so we need to be patient and persevere. There is no pressure to ace this, as we are all beginners when just starting out. Just commit to the practice. Most importantly, never judge yourself harshly for the difficulties that may arise. These are a normal part of the process.

It is quite evident that choosing the suitable technique and meditation is key for the success of one's practice. Not every soul is energized by the same tunes. We need to choose one practice, stick with it for a while and if it is not working for us, discard it and try something different. We each search within our own hearts in order to find what draws us closest to our Source.

As we bravely open up to explore our deepest depths, each of us should be empowered to follow our unique path with all the strength of being there is.

///////////////////////////////////

GLOSSARY
HEBREW WORDS & TERMS

Ayin: *Emptiness, no-thing-ness, The Unmanifest*

AriZal: *Acronym for, "The Lion, Rabbi Yitzchak (Isaac) (Luria) of blessed memory" (1534-1572). The father of contemporary Kabbalah. His teachings are referred to as Lurianic Kabbalah.*

Bereishis: *The first book of the Torah (the five books of Moses), otherwise known as Genesis.*

Boded: *Being alone.*

Baal Shem: *Literally, Master of the Name. A Baal Shem was a mystical healer, mostly using amulets. The most well-known Baal Shem was Rabbi Yisrael (Israel) Baal Shem Tov.*

Baal Shem Tov: *Master of the Good Name. The mystic and Rabbi Yisrael (Israel) son of Eliezer (1698-1760). The legendary founder of the Chassidic movement.*

Chesed: *The act of loving-kindness. Expansiveness and giving.*

Deviekus: *Cleaving, being unified. The spiritual sensation of being one with G-d.*

Gevurah: *The act of holding back, withdrawing. Inwardness and restriction.*

Hashem: *Literally, "The Name". Hashem is said instead of the Tetragrammaton, the predominant name of G-d in the Torah. This name of G-d is written with four Hebrew letters, the Yud-Hei-Vav-Hei. Being that this name is not pronounced, it is simply called "The Name".*

Hisbodedus: *The spiritual practice of being alone. Also known as the practice of speaking to the Creator openly, as one would converse with their best friend.*

Hislahavus: *Open and displayed emotions, excitement.*

Kavanah: *Intention. Focused mindfulness.*

Maggid of Mezritch: *Rabbi DovBer (? - 1772), the primary student and accepted successor of the Baal Shem Tov.*

Medrash: *Rabbinic writings of allegory and narrative, often containing the 'behind the scenes' stories that fill out the Biblical narrative; part of the oral tradition of Torah.*

Mitzvah: *The commandments of the Torah, also understood as good deeds, ritual obligations or actions that connect the doer with his deepest self and with his Creator.*

Musar: *An ethical, educational and cultural movement that developed in the 19th century in Eastern Europe, particularly among Lithuanian Jews.*

Rambam: *Acronym for Rabbi Moshe Ben Maimon, also known as Maimonides (1135- 1204), the great Jewish Spanish rational philosopher.*

Ralbag: *Acronym for Rabbi Levi Ben Gershon, also known as Gersonides (1288–1344), a French philosopher, Talmudist, mathematician and astronomer.*

Ratzu: *A desire to expire in spiritual bliss. To run. To reach upwards.*

Rebbe: *Chassidic master and teacher in the style and spiritual tradition of the Baal Shem Tov*

Sefirah or Sefiros: *The 'vessels' or 'lenses' that refract and reflect the Infinite Light in order so that it can manifest within the finite, created reality; a series of cosmic/consciousness transducers that help to transform Infinite Light into finite form.*

Shechinah: *The Divine presence within creation. The feminine indwelling presence of G-d.*

Shuv: *Return. The awareness that the purpose of life is within the here and now.*

Tzimtzum: *The (apparent) Divine withdrawal. The contraction of the Infinite Light to make room for finitude.*

Tzadik (plural: **Tzadikim**): *A righteous person. Also, refers to a spiritual master, miracle worker, or Rebbe*

Talmud: *The Collected Rabbinic writings that contain Halacha, "law", and Agadah, "lore". Part of the oral tradition of the Torah.*

Torah: *Generally refers to the Bible, the Five Books of Moses. In broader definition, this term includes the entire canon of Jewish thought.*

Yesh: *A something. Individual, separate existence.*

Yichud: *Unification. Unifying a physical action with a spiritual intention.*

Zohar: *Primary, multi-volume work of Kabbalah. Teachings date back to the 1st century sage Rabbi Shimon Bar Yochai. Published and made public in 1290's.*

OTHER BOOKS
BY RAV DOVBER PINSON

REINCARNATION AND JUDAISM
The Journey of the Soul

A fascinating analysis of the concept of reincarnation as it appears in the works of the Kabbalistic masters, as well as how it is discussed by the great thinkers throughout history. Dipping into the fountain of ancient wisdom and modern understanding, the book addresses and answers such basic questions as: What is reincarnation? Why does it occur? And how does it affect us personally?

INNER RHYTHMS
The Kabbalah of Music

Exploring the inner dimension of sound and music, and particularly, how music permeates all aspects of life. The topics range from Deveikus/ Unity, Yichudim/ Unifications, to the more personal issues, such as Simcha/Happiness, and Marirus/ sadness.

MEDITATION AND JUDAISM
Exploring the Jewish Meditative Paths

A comprehensive work on Jewish meditation, encompassing the entire spectrum of Jewish thought--from the early
Kabbalists to the modern Chassidic and Mussar masters,
the sages of the Talmud to the modern philosophers. The
book is both a scholarly, in-depth study of meditative practices, and a practical, easy to follow guide for any person
interested in meditating the Jewish way. In addition, the
book broadens our view of meditation, demonstrating that
in addition to the traditional methods of meditation, meditation is prevalent within so many of the common Jewish
practices.

TOWARD THE INFINITE
The Way of Kabbalistic Meditation

A book focusing exclusively on the Kabbalistic – Chassidic, Hisbonenus approach to meditation. Encompassing the
entire meditative experience, it takes the reader on a comprehensive and engaging journey through meditation. The
book explores the various states of consciousness that a person encounters in the course of the meditation, beginning
at a level of extreme self-awareness and concluding with a
total state of non-awareness.

JEWISH WISDOM OF THE AFTERLIFE
The Myths, the Mysteries & Meanings

What happens to us after we physically die? What is consciousness? And can it survive without a physical brain? What is a soul? Can we remember our past lives? Do near-death-experiences prove the immortality of the soul? Drawing from the fountain of ancient Jewish wisdom and modern understanding of what consciousness is, this book explores the possibilities of surviving death, the near-death-experience, and a possible glimpse of the peace and unconditional love that awaits, empowering the reader to live their day-to-day life with these great spiritual truths.

UPSHERIN
Exploring the Laws, Customs & Meanings
of a Boy's First Haircut

What is the meaning of Upsherin, the traditional celebration of a boy's first haircut at the age of three? This in-depth answer to that question explores as well the questions: Why is a boy's hair allowed to grow freely for his first three years? What is the kabbalistic import of hair in all its lengths and varieties? What is the mystical meaning of hair coverings? Rav Pinson answers these questions with his trademark deep learning and spiritual sensitivity. Includes a guide to conducting an Upsherin ceremony.

THIRTY-TWO GATES OF WISDOM
Awakening through Kabbalah

Kabbalah holds the secrets to a path of conscious awareness. In this compact book, Rav Pinson presents 32 key
concepts of Kabbalah and shows their value in opening the
gates of perception.

THE PURIM READER
The Holiday of Purim Explored

With a Persian name, a costuming dress code and a woman as the heroine, Purim is certainly unusual amongst the
Jewish holidays. Most people are very familiar with the
costumes, Megilah and revelry, but are mystified by their
significance. Rav Pinson offers a glimpse into the unknown
world of Purim, uncovering the mysteries and offering a
deeper understanding of this unique holiday.

EIGHT LIGHTS
8 Meditations for Chanukah

What is the meaning and message of Chanukah? What
is the spiritual significance of the Lights of the Menorah?
What are the Lights telling us? What is the deeper dimen-

sion of the Dreidel? Rav Pinson, with his trademark deep learning and spiritual sensitivity guides us through eight meditations relating to the Lights of the Menorah and the eight days of Chanukah, and a deeper exploration of the Dreidel.

Includes a detailed how-to guide for lighting the Chanukah Menorah

....

THE IYYUN HAGADAH
An Introduction to the Haggadah

In this beautifully written introduction to Passover and the Haggadah, Rav DovBer Pinson, guides us through the major themes of Passover and the Seder night. Rav Pinson addresses the important questions, such as: What is the big deal of Chametz? What are we trying to achieve through conducting a Seder? What's with all that stuff on the Seder Plate? And most importantly, how is this all related to freedom? His answers will surprise even those who think they already know the answers to these questions.

....

THE MYSTERY OF KADDISH
Understanding the Mourner's Kaddish

The Mystery of Kaddish is an in-depth and Kabbalistic exploration into the Mourner's Kaddish Prayer. Throughout

Jewish history, there have been many rites and rituals associated with loss and mourning, yet none have prevailed quite like the Mourner's Kaddish Prayer - which has become the definitive ritual of mourning. The book explores the source of this prayer and deconstructs the meaning to better understand the grieving process and how the Kaddish prayer supports and uplifts the bereaved through their own personal journey to healing.

RECLAIMING THE SELF
The Way of Teshuvah

Teshuvah is one of the great gifts of life. It speaks of a hope for a better today and empowers us to choose a brighter tomorrow. But what exactly is Teshuvah? And how does it work? How can we undo our past and how do we deal with guilt? And what is healthy regret without eroding our self-esteem? In this fascinating and empowering book, world-renowned teacher and thinker, Rav DovBer Pinson lays out a path for genuine transformation and a way to include all of our past in the powerful moment of the now.

PASSPORT TO KABBALAH
A Journey of Inner Transformation

Life is a journey full of ups and downs, inside-outs, and unexpected detours. There are times when we think we know exactly where we want to be headed, and other times when we are so lost we don't even know where we are. Rooted in the teachings of Kabbalah, this book provides readers with a passport of sorts to help them through any obstacles along their path of self-refinement, reflection, and self-transformation.

....

THE FOUR SPECIES
The Symbolism of the Lulav & Esrog

The Four Species have inspired countless commentaries and traditions and intrigued scholars and mystics alike. In this little masterpiece of wisdom both profound and practical - Rav DovBer Pinson explores the deep symbolic roots and nature of the Four Species. The Na'anuim, or ritual of the Lulav movement, is meticulously detailed and Kavanos, or meditations, are offered for use with the practice. Includes an illustrated guide to the Lulav Movements.

....

A BOND FOR ETERNITY
Understanding the Bris Milah

What is the Bris Milah – the covenant through circumcision? What does it represent, symbolize and signify? An in depth and sensitive review of this fundamental Mitzvah. In this little masterpiece of wisdom ¬—profound yet accessible, Rav Pinson reveals the deeper meaning of this essential rite of passage and its eternal link to the Jewish people.

....

THE GARDEN OF PARADOX:
The Essence of Non Dual Kabbalah

This book is a Primer on the Essential Philosophy of Kabbalah, presented as a series of 3 conversations, revealing the mysteries of Creator, Creation and Consciousness. With three representational students, embodying respectively, the philosopher, the activist and the mystic, Rav Pinson tackles the larger questions of life. Who is G-d? Who am I? Why do I exist? What is my purpose in this life? Written in clear and concise prose, Rav Pinson gently guides the reader towards making sense of life's paradoxes and living meaningfully.

....

WRAPPED IN MAJESTY
Tefillin- Exploring the Mystery

Tefillin, the black boxes and leather straps that are worn during prayer, are curiously powerful and mysterious. Within the inky black boxes lie untold secrets. In this profound, passionate and thought-provoking text, Rav Pinson explores and reveals the multi-dimensional perspectives of

Tefillin. Magically weaving together all dimensions of To-rah;, Peshat, literal observation, to Remez, the allegorical; Derush, the homiletic, to Sod, hidden Kabbalistic, into one wonderful tapestry. Inspirational and instructive, Wrapped in Majesty: Tefillin, will make putting on the Tefillin more meaningful and deepen the experience.

....

INNER WORLDS OF JEWISH PRAYER
A Guide to Develop and Deepen Your Prayer Experience

An in depth exploration and explanation of the actual Inner Experience of prayer. What occurs or could occur, when we pray? And how do we enter into a prayerful posture or modality? With practical step-by-step wisdom on walking the path of meaningful and transformative prayer

ABOUT THE AUTHOR

RAV DOVBER PINSON is a world-renowned Torah scholar, Kabbalist, prolific author and beloved spiritual teacher. He is widely recognized as one of the world's foremost authorities on authentic Kabbalah and Jewish wisdom.

Through his books, lectures and wise counsel he has touched and inspired the lives of thousands the world over.

Rav Pinson travels extensively teaching and lecturing and his books have been translated into Hebrew, German, Spanish, Russian and Portuguese.

Rav Pinson resides in Brooklyn, NY and is the Rosh Yeshivah of the IYYUN Yeshiva in Downtown Brooklyn and Dean of IYYUN International Center for Jewish Study.

CPSIA information can be obtained
at www.ICGtesting.com
Printed in the USA
BVHW030605230620
581993BV00006B/365

9 780989 007214